How to ~~Survive~~ Love Your
Retirement

WARNING:

This guide contains differing opinions. Hundreds of Heads will not always agree. Advice taken in combination may cause unwanted side effects. Use your head when selecting advice.

How to ~~survive~~ *Love* Your
Retirement

Advice From Hundreds of Retirees

BARBARA WAXMAN, M.S., M.P.A.
ROBERT A. MENDELSON, M.D., F.A.A.P.
SPECIAL EDITORS

HUNDREDS OF HEADS BOOKS, LLC
Atlanta, Georgia

Illustrations © 2006 by Image Club
Cover photograph by PictureQuest
Cover and Book design by Elizabeth Johnsboen

Library of Congress Cataloging-in-Publication Data
How to love your retirement/by hundreds who stopped working and started living (and some who kept working but had more fun); Barbara Waxman and Robert A. Mendelson, special editors.
    p. cm.
ISBN-13: 978-0-9746292-7-8
ISBN-10: 0-9746292-7-8
  1. Retirement—United States. 2. Retirees—United States—Life skills guides. I. Waxman, Barbara Frey. II. Mendelson, Robert A.
  HQ1063.2U6 H68
  646.7'90973—dc22

                                              2005021219

See pages 201-202 for credits and permissions.

HUNDREDS OF HEADS® books are available at special discounts when purchased in bulk for premiums or institutional or educational use. Excerpts and custom editions can be created for specific uses. For more information, please email sales@hundredsofheads.com or write to:

HUNDREDS OF HEADS BOOKS, LLC
#230
2221 Peachtree Road, Suite D
Atlanta, Georgia 30309

ISBN-10: 0-9746292-7-8
ISBN-13: 978-09746292-7-8

Printed in U.S.A.
10 9 8 7 6 5 4 3

CONTENTS

Here's a little secret: There is no such thing as retirement anymore! Concluding your full-time career doesn't mean being "put out to pasture." On the contrary, it's an opportunity to begin a whole new and exciting phase of your life.

When retirement was created (yes, it was created!), people were only expected to live for about 10 more years, and not all of those very robustly, at that. A lifestyle of leisure became the accepted American way to drift off into the sunset. People wouldn't get tired of it because it wouldn't last all that long.

Now, people live longer. Retirees today may face two decades or more of productive time. Unlike any other time in our nation's history, we are in the midst of a revolution. Over the next 40 years, the 50-and-older population will grow 68 times faster than the general population. There will be more than 86.7 million people over the age of 65 in the United States by 2050. And not only are there more older adults than ever, but they are healthier, better educated, and more active than ever before. Disability figures associated with age are declining—there are already 70,000 centenarians, and as many as 3 million baby boomers are expected to live to 100!

So how can you make this next phase the best chapter of your life? At Hundreds of Heads Books, we believe that when you are facing any challenging life experience, it's good to get ideas and advice from others who have already done so. *How to Love Your Retirement* offers you the wisdom of hundreds of people who have gone before you and made the most of this stage of their lives.

This new retirement (some call it *protirement*) will be a creation all your own. It's worth repeating that retirement no longer means giving up work: Plenty of people who officially retired from their main job still work, often full time. Some still choose to take it easy at home, work, or pursue hobbies part-time, or travel. Some of the happiest people we interviewed found a way to use their extra time to pursue other passions: A baseball fan got a job at the ballpark; a ski buff took a winter job at a mountain resort; a journalist started a business creating oral histories. The key word is choice: How will you choose to navigate these new waters? How would you prefer to live this next chapter (we call it the "third age") of your life?

This book intends to offer you guidance—not only from the perspectives of retirees from all over the country, but also through resources, tips, and exercises designed to help you access your own answers and map your own journey.

Retirement used to be defined for us, but not any more. Find the wisdom that works for you and enjoy your time. You've earned it!

BARBARA WAXMAN
M.S., M.P.A.

My role as a special editor for a book about retirement gives me a wonderful opportunity: After all, I have been working or going to school, or both, for 60 years. Looking back (or in any other direction), that's a long time, with a lot of experiences to share!

I entered pediatric medical practice at the age of 30. My wife and I had three children at the time and one more to come. At that time, I wasn't even thinking about retirement; the daunting task of raising and educating four children was much more immediate.

But during the next few decades, I began to think about how I could afford to work less than full time without giving up our relatively comfortable lifestyle. I was fortunate to develop a relationship with a very wise man who became a friend, mentor, and financial adviser. I took care of his children, and he took care of my future. It was a good trade-off!

At age 65, and as senior partner of the pediatric practice, I decided that I could finally afford to cut down to about half the time and half the income. It was a turning point in my life, both professionally and personally. A few years later, my wife of 46 years was diagnosed with an unexpected illness that required all of her time and much of mine. I cut back even further and eventually retired from practice. That decision was made for me. There were no options. During that time, I sought advice from many friends and associates, and it has helped me immensely.

The Hundreds of Heads approach is a splendid one for teaching and learning. Throughout my life, whenever I had a dilemma, I sought advice and counsel from people who have "been there" and "done that."

Having the opportunity to read hundreds of opinions about retirement has been unique, educational, and entertaining. I hope readers of this book feel the same way, and that they will get many ideas that could contribute to a "happier ever after."

ROBERT A. MENDELSON
M.D., F.A.A.P.

50 and Counting: Is It Time to Retire?

It's been in the back of your mind for much of your working life: retirement, the finish line. It's at once exciting and frightening. Soon you'll get to spend your days doing only what you please. But are you really ready to call an end to your career? How do you know when you're able to let go of the working world and live life on your own schedule? Are your finances in shape? Equally important, are you and your spouse emotionally in agreement? We've asked others how they knew it was time. Here's how they handled the first step in their new lives.

RETIRE WHILE YOU'RE STILL YOUNG ENOUGH TO HANDLE IT. I just retired, and packing up our house right now is exhausting me. I can only do it for certain amounts of time each day.

—BRENDA JUSTICE
WICHITA, KANSAS
YEARS RETIRED: 1

* * * * * * * *

I HAD BEEN THINKING ABOUT RETIREMENT FOR SOME TIME, but really couldn't make up my mind to quit a job I truly loved. My relationships with my students meant so much to me that I was afraid I'd miss them terribly if I retired. I thought about it and prayed about it. Finally, God got tired of listening to me and gave me a shove. I lost my voice; for a teacher, that can be disastrous. I thought I had laryngitis, but found out it was something else and that it wasn't going to clear up on its own. Now, after three years of regular treatment, I have my voice back most of the time. God knew what I needed, even if I didn't.

—SUSAN
TAYLOR, TEXAS
YEARS RETIRED: 3

* * * * * * * *

THE RIGHT TIME TO RETIRE IS WHEN you have more things to do outside of work than you have time to do while working.

—YITZ
MANCHESTER, UNITED KINGDOM
YEARS RETIRED: 8

WHEN YOU HAVE ENOUGH MONEY TO LIVE for the rest of your life without working, that's when you know it's time to retire. For some people, that might be when they're 30. Others might not hit this point until they're 93. For me, it happened in my 60s.

—GARY GALLAGHER
WILLIAMSON, WEST VIRGINIA
YEARS RETIRED: 1

. . . .

A PERSON KNOWS. When it became a seven-day-a-week job for me, not five, I knew I was ready. If you take pride in what you do, and if you think you can no longer give the job what you need, it's time.

—H.I.H.
DURHAM, NORTH CAROLINA
YEARS RETIRED: 7

. . . .

I WAS A PEDIATRIC NURSE-PRACTITIONER FOR 25 YEARS, and before I turned 60, I thought I would work until I was 90. I loved my job so much! After I turned 60, I found I was just getting so tired. Sixty really seems to be a turning point for people, a time when they really start thinking about retirement. So I decided to retire and was able to phase myself out over a six-month period.

—CYNTHIA
ST. PAUL, MINNESOTA
YEARS RETIRED: 8

BY THE AGE OF 65, MOST OF US have accomplished whatever work-related goals we are going to reach. If you haven't done it by then, chances are you aren't going to do it. Take the retirement, take the pension, take the Social Security, and sail off into the sunset.

— SUE LASKY
POLAND, OHIO

* * * * * * * *

I DID NOT GET MUCH CHOICE ON MY RETIREMENT. They came to me when I was 59 1/2 and told me that if I didn't retire, they were going to take away about $40,000 a year in pay. I had planned to stay until I was 62, but I couldn't afford not to go.

— LAWRENCE "BIMP" LAYMAN
HARRISONBURG, VIRGINIA
YEARS RETIRED: 1

* * * * * * * *

I KNEW I WANTED TO HAVE A CERTAIN LIFESTYLE when I retired, and I sat down with a financial planner who gave us a very good list to think about what we spend money on. It really helped. You just have to focus, think about what you are going to do, what kind of finances you need, and do it.

— E.M.
EDGEWATER, NEW JERSEY
YEARS RETIRED: 3

WHEN IS THE RIGHT AGE TO RETIRE? When you dread going to work.

—MARY BRIGHT
ALLENTOWN, PENNSYLVANIA
YEARS RETIRED: 10

* * * * * * * *

PLAN AHEAD

If retirement is on your horizon, come up with a list of post-retirement activities in advance and, if necessary, take time *before* you retire to acquire skills you can use in your post-retirement life.

* * * * * * * *

TWO YEARS BEFORE I WANTED TO RETIRE, my company informed me that it no longer needed my job. As part of my severance package, I received one month's salary for every year of employment. Altogether, this amounted to 18 months of pay. In contrast, if I'd continued working for those two years and retired on my own terms, I would've received nothing. Sometimes, it really is better to retire according to your company's schedule!

—ANONYMOUS
CORVALLIS, OREGON
YEARS RETIRED: 11

TO CELEBRATE YOUR RETIREMENT, just be with the people you love.

—ALLAN S. ROSS
SAN ANTONIO, TEXAS
YEARS RETIRED: 1

• • • • • • • •

MAKE THE MOST OUT OF YOUR WORKING YEARS

According to a study by the Employee Benefit Research Institute, Minnesota has the highest level of participation in employment-based retirement plans. Florida, Georgia, and California came in last.

• • • • • • • •

MY BROTHER WENT INTO THE HOSPITAL FOR ROUTINE SURGERY. He got an infection and died a few weeks later. His sudden death made my husband and me realize that we were getting older. We wanted to spend time together and have fun while we were healthy. He was the one who suggested that we retire, but I agreed. It was the best decision we could have made. We love not having to get up and go to work.

—DONNA HANAFIN
NIXA, MISSOURI

I FIGURED IF I WAITED NINE MORE YEARS UNTIL I TURNED 65, I wouldn't be able to do some of the things I could do at 56. These extra years have given my husband and me valuable extra time to see the country and do things we were never able to do before.

—G.M.
CUMBERLAND, MARYLAND
YEARS RETIRED: 4

* * * * * * * *

RETIRE SOONER RATHER THAN LATER. Do not let financial issues dictate when you retire. Let your excitement for the job dictate when you leave it. If you are burned out, hating the job, or too stressed, leave it and get another job if you have to. Work part-time if you can't afford to completely retire. The stress of a job that you're not enjoying will have physical effects on the body.

—FRANK HAWK
LAKELAND, FLORIDA
YEARS RETIRED: 3

* * * * * * * *

I DID NOT PLAN FOR RETIREMENT IN ANY ORGANIZED WAY. I just thought that retirement would give me time to travel and time to take the Master Gardener training course, which I had long wanted to do.

—ANONYMOUS
NEVADA
YEARS RETIRED: 13

LIKE NIKE SAYS, "JUST DO IT." It's the best thing I ever did for myself.

—BRADLEY IMHOF
HARRISONBURG, VIRGINIA
YEARS RETIRED: 1

* * * * * * *

DEFINING *RETIREMENT:* "Do nothing, receive money."

—BILL STRAIN
KERRVILLE, TEXAS
YEARS RETIRED: 6

* * * * * * *

I WAS IN THE CAR ABOUT SEVEN YEARS AGO with my younger sister. She and her husband had just retired, and I'm thinking, "Why am I still working my buns off?" I said, "How can I retire?" and I pulled the car over and made her get out a pencil and some paper, and we began to write down all my assets and what they were worth. I've always been good with budgets, so we began to form one: She wrote down food, insurance, doctor bills, mortgages, and what they cost monthly, then subtracted the mortgages (since I planned to sell my real estate company to pay off my house). And that moment, I finally realized, "Hey, I can do this." It took place in that car and from that day, I really planned. It took about a year to make it happen—to sell the business and pay off our home mortgage. Once the pressure of mortgage payments was gone, it was so easy.

—BARBARA STEVENS
GATLINBURG, TENNESSEE
YEARS RETIRED: 6

MY CAREER IN EDUCATION ESTABLISHED a fixed pension based on 34 years of service, which gave me full benefits. Things like health insurance, Roth IRAs, tax-sheltered annuities, and daughters getting married are not fixed items, but they all are certainly a part of the decision. I retired at age 58, but knew I was ready to retire several years before. Planning was essential, and that is probably the number one skill I learned in my profession—plan ahead!

—DEE
OAK LAWN, ILLINOIS
YEARS RETIRED: 1

* * * * * * * *

THE NEXT WAVE

Experts project a major wave of retirement starting in 2011, when the first baby boomers turn 65.

* * * * * * * *

MY SITUATION IS A LITTLE DIFFERENT THAN MOST: I am retired from the military. I put in my 20 years and then got the heck out. When I tell people I'm retired, they look at me funny because I'm only 46.

—TAMMY NELSON
MIDLOTHIAN, MARYLAND
YEARS RETIRED: 3

THE NUMBER ONE THING IS TO MAKE UP YOUR MIND that you're retiring when you do. Know that it is a very significant step and make it permanent—don't dabble in going back. If you keep trying to touch back into what you did, even if you are volunteering, you'll find fault in how your job is now being done.

—MARGARET MCCOWN
JACKSONVILLE, TEXAS
YEARS RETIRED: 16

I WOULD HAVE LIKED TO RETIRE GRADUALLY, but as a nurse in a hospital, all the technological changes and procedures became overwhelming. I was very relieved when I quit. If you can retire gradually, it will be much more enjoyable. As you age, you lose energy and get tired, and you realize that you can't do everything.

—J.L.
MINNEAPOLIS, MINNESOTA
YEARS RETIRED: 10

I FIGURED 46 YEARS OF WORK WAS ENOUGH FOR ONE LIFETIME. I wanted to see what else I could do with my time. What I wanted to do more than anything else was tend to my garden. That's my real passion. I wish I could have gotten paid to do that. Now I tell people I'm a full-time gardener working for the best boss in the world—me.

—P.Y.
BARRELVILLE, MARYLAND
YEARS RETIRED: 4

I RETIRED IN DECEMBER OF 1996, and it was the best thing that ever happened to me. My company was cutting back, and I was about the oldest person there, so I went to my boss and told him that if they were offering severance packages, I'd take one. I was 60 then.

—JANIS
CARY, NORTH CAROLINA
YEARS RETIRED: 8

* * * * * * * *

A GOOD FRIEND OF MINE ONCE SAID, "You'll know when the time comes." For me, I was having health problems. But also, my whole office had been computerized, and it was a struggle for me. I couldn't even type! It was my time.

—JOHN R. BRIGHT
ALLENTOWN, PENNSYLVANIA
YEARS RETIRED: 10

* * * * * * * *

I PROBABLY NEVER WOULD HAVE RETIRED if I hadn't started dating a new boyfriend who had a house up in New Hampshire. I felt like I was getting older, and I was having such a good time with him. I wanted to enjoy going up there together, which was tough with the amount of vacation you get in life. I'm sure if I had said something to my boss, I could have worked a couple of days a week, but I loved going up for the whole summer, and I don't think that would have been possible.

—SONYA
BROOKLYN, NEW YORK
YEARS RETIRED: 10

PARTY TIME

Every rite of passage deserves celebration. Including retirement.
You deserve to be rewarded for all those years of hard work (and
celebrate the fact that you'll no longer be doing it). Here's how
others made the most of their newfound freedom.

I TOLD TWO PERSONAL STORIES WHEN I spoke at my retirement party. One was very funny, and the other one was
extremely meaningful to the people who worked at the
hospital I was retiring from. Try to tell a personal story that
is really meaningful that happened to you at the institution. It will resonate with people you are saying goodbye
to. We're all trying to find meaning in life.
It's good to tell a funny story, too.

—ROY CLARY
BROOKLYN, NEW YORK
YEARS RETIRED: 1

• • • • • • • •

MAKE SURE THAT PEOPLE ARE well aware of your post-
retirement plans when you have a retirement party. At my
retirement party, we had big signs that listed all the places
I wanted to go in retirement. It gave us all something to
talk about. It felt like people weren't saying goodbye but
were saying, "Bon voyage … we'll see you when you get
back!"

—AARON
ST. PETERSBURG, FLORIDA
YEARS RETIRED: 2

ON MY FIRST DAY OF RETIREMENT, I slept late, ate brunch out, and then just slouched around the house all day with my guys (dog and husband). This was after joyriding during the hot summer day at noontime with the sunroof open, the windows down, and the radio blaring, just because we could.

> —C.R.
> SAN ANTONIO, TEXAS
> YEARS RETIRED: 1

* * * * * * * *

WHEN THE SUBJECT OF MY RETIREMENT PARTY CAME UP, I told people in my department that if I had to choose, I would choose not to have one. People in the department said, "We don't care whether you come or not. We're having one." Just take it all in and enjoy it. My retirement party had about 100 people. The secretaries in the department were the primary organizers. They wrote to several colleagues and asked for letters, which were included in the book that was given to me. They had pictures of me over time that showed that we do, indeed, get older. They invited all of my children and stepchildren. They all said nice things. My wife was there to greet people with me. The department gave me some small gifts and humorous gifts. There were snacks and a cake and punch. It was a very nice affair.

> —ROBERT L. ZIMDAHL
> FORT COLLINS, COLORADO
> YEARS RETIRED: 1

I WAS OFFERED AN INCENTIVE PLAN TO RETIRE that included a half year of pay. I was 63 years old. I started working when I was nine years old, sweeping at the local grocery store before school. I worked hard all of my life; I decided it was time to enjoy it. You should take advantage of the opportunity to do the things you love while you are in good health.

—JOHN BECKER
SPRINGFIELD, MISSOURI
YEARS RETIRED: 12

* * * * * * * *

I RETIRED BECAUSE I WAS BURNED OUT. We had this business conference down in Ames, Iowa, and it was with a bunch of young businessmen. They had the fancy suits and the big cars, but they didn't really understand the business. Listening to those baboons, I just decided I didn't want to do it anymore. I sat there for a day and a half, thinking the whole time about retirement, figuring out if I could do it financially.

—JIMBO
MINNEAPOLIS, MINNESOTA
YEARS RETIRED: 14

* * * * * * * *

I WANTED TO TOTALLY CHANGE MY LIFE AROUND. They say you have a new life waiting, and I wanted to be young enough to enjoy it.

—J.L.
JACKSON, NEW JERSEY
YEARS RETIRED: 2

WHEN YOU FINALLY GET SICK OF ALL THE BS, it's time to retire. As an assistant principal, I wanted to make certain changes. Specifically, I wanted to involve the community with our school by developing more family-oriented activities. Unfortunately, there were all these roadblocks (read: other people) who wouldn't allow it. I simply didn't have the energy to fight anymore. I'd been working for 32 years, and I knew retirement was just around the corner anyway, so I figured, why not do it now?

—JEFFREY WACO
NEW YORK, NEW YORK
YEARS RETIRED: 2

* * * * * * * *

I RETIRED COLD TURKEY. I was tired of the structured work environment after 40 years and wanted a clean break. I am tempted to say that maybe I should have worked for another three years, until 65, but this would have been just to save more money and draw a higher Social Security check. And I would have found those additional three years a real grind.

—B.L.
SAN JOSE, CALIFORNIA
YEARS RETIRED: 8

* * * * * * * *

I DON'T THINK THERE IS A SINGLE BEST AGE for someone to retire. I think that it's as individual as we are.

—SUSAN
TAYLOR, TEXAS
YEARS RETIRED: 3

I WORKED IN CONSTRUCTION MY WHOLE LIFE, and the work just got to be too much for me physically. That's really a younger man's work, but it was the only thing I ever did and the only thing I knew how to do. After I turned 50, I really started to feel the aches and pains more frequently. At the end of each week, I'd really be hurting. Luckily, I had saved enough money and my wife has a good enough job that I could call it quits.

—Ray Vincet
LaVale, Maryland
Years retired: 3

* * * * * * *

THIRTY WAS MY MAGIC NUMBER. Once I hit 30 years of service, I was outta there.

—Karen Weaver
Lancaster, Pennsylvania
Years retired: 2

* * * * * * *

WE STARTED PLANNING FOR RETIREMENT TWO YEARS before we did it. We explored, looking for a place we would want to settle. Weather was a factor: We had a great vacation home in Maine where we liked to spend the summer, but in the winter, there was usually about 20 feet of snow, and that wasn't something that seemed appealing. We found some land in Seattle and started the building process. We retired, moved in, and did the finishing work ourselves.

—George Ries
Seattle, Washington
Years retired: 30

I HAD BEEN TEACHING 36 YEARS, and I was just going through the motions. I met with a financial consultant about retirement planning and found out that I'd be taking home more money after retiring. My paycheck now is larger; it was a great opportunity!

—Daniel DiMatteo
Miller Place, New York
Years retired: 4

* * * * * * *

I WAS GOING TO CONTINUE WORKING A LITTLE LONGER, but then things changed suddenly: The universe wanted me out sooner. I was having problems with my heart. I didn't really feel like there was much of a choice. I could have stayed a little longer, but I decided that, rather than waiting and leaving because of health issues a few months down the road, I should at least embrace where I was being sent next. Either way, the universe was going to get me where I am now: retirement. It's important for people to acknowledge when there are forces greater than their conscious minds affecting their decisions, and to realize there's no way to fight them.

—Michael
Sayville, New York
Years retired: 1

* * * * * * *

RETIRE AS SOON AS YOU CAN DO IT FINANCIALLY.
Don't be a hero. Enjoy the time you have left.

—Dom Greco
Poland, Ohio

I WAS ONLY 42 WHEN I RETIRED, so I bought 80 acres and started raising cattle.

—MENDELL PETER SPARKS
SPRINGFIELD, MISSOURI
YEARS RETIRED: 15

* * * * * * * *

HOW DID I KNOW WHEN IT WAS TIME TO RETIRE? My wife told me! I was teaching at a university in San Angelo, Texas. My wife took a teaching job in El Paso. For about two years we commuted back and forth on the weekends; it was about a six-and-a-half-hour drive. I knew it was time to retire when my wife said, "I've been following you around for 30 years! Now it's time for you to follow me!" So I retired from my university job and moved to El Paso.

—ANONYMOUS
EL PASO, TEXAS
YEARS RETIRED: 2

* * * * * * * *

AFTER YOU RETIRE, ALLOW YOURSELF TO VEG OUT for at least three months after leaving the busy working world. Just hang out. Don't make any specific plans; be spontaneous and do what you feel like doing. Give the things in your heart time to bubble up and help you decide what your priorities will be in your retirement years. Decide what means the most to you and what you really feel passionate about. Then go for it big-time.

—EMILY KIMBALL
RICHMOND, VIRGINIA

RETIREMENT SOUNDS SO TERMINAL. It's really the end of one part of life and the beginning of another. It's a transition from part one to part two. Some people do it gradually. When I knew I was going to retire a year ago, I already felt like I was retired, so I was trying out things like playing with investments and hobbies.

—GARY SMITH
SAN ANTONIO, TEXAS
YEARS RETIRED: 1

* * * * * * * *

I WAS TEMPORARILY RETIRED WHEN I suffered an injury and had to give up my dental practice. At this time, the enforced schedule resulted in a complete relaxation of my previously uptight personality. For the first time in my life, I was not under pressure to produce an income that would support the household. Because it was out of my hands, and I had no choice, I was able to use the time to unwind and focus on the things I really enjoyed. In a way, it was a blessing.

—ANONYMOUS
TORONTO, ONTARIO
YEARS RETIRED: 10

* * * * * * * *

MY DECISION TO RETIRE WAS PARTLY HEALTH-RELATED. After going through breast cancer surgery, I no longer know what my life expectancy is. I want to enjoy whatever time I have left now while I still can.

—KATHY
WASHINGTON, D.C.
YEARS RETIRED: 1

IT IS UNWISE TO THINK YOU CAN PLAN YOUR RETIREMENT with any exactitude. Unexpected events crop up, and sometimes you have to change course a bit. But don't sweat it; go with the flow.

—B.L.
SAN JOSE, CALIFORNIA
YEARS RETIRED: 8

* * * * * * * *

I RETIRED WHEN I WAS 60, which is really quite a luxury. I was able to access some of my retirement funds, and my husband, who had been working part-time, was really ready to retire. Also, I wanted to have time to spend with my mother; we ended up having three years when we could go shopping every week, and I'm so glad I was able to do that. And finally, I felt like I was going out at the top of my game, not when I was sick of the job and all my coworkers.

—JEANNE
MINNEAPOLIS, MINNESOTA
YEARS RETIRED: 7

The "R" Word: What Do You Mean, "Retire"?

Retirement is relative. Human beings have a capacity to be productive with their days, and after all those years of work, some people find it impossible to just stop being … human. The result? Some go back to work. Some use the experiences they have gained in the real world to start their own businesses. And some try to make the world a better place through volunteering. Wondering what you'll do after retirement? Fear not: There's plenty of work to go around.

I NEVER HEARD OF THE WORD RETIREMENT. I know my father never heard of that word, and that's probably why I'm not familiar with it. What exactly does that mean? I picture a bunch of old geezers sitting around playing gin rummy in rocking chairs with afghans over their laps: No, thank you. That's not for me. I plan to get up every day and get my hands dirty until God calls me home.

—MITZIE HAGEN
WHEELING, WEST VIRGINIA
YEARS RETIRED: 4

* * * * * * * *

IF YOU'RE GOING TO RETIRE, you need activities to keep you sharp. My plan was to open a kayak-touring business based out of a family vacation home in New Hampshire. It has been a little more difficult than I expected, but I'm doing it. And I've found it's nice to have something to do for six months a year.

—FRED
MILLER PLACE, NEW YORK
YEARS RETIRED: 2

* * * * * * * *

THE ONE THING THAT HAS SURPRISED ME about retirement is how many people I see not working. We'll go to town to eat or shop during the day, and I see so many people who are retired or just piddling that it makes me wonder: Who is supporting this country?

—JIM EYRE
JACKSONVILLE, TEXAS
YEARS RETIRED: 6

HAVING WORK KEEPS YOU INVOLVED WITH PEOPLE. You wake up every morning knowing you've got something to do. When you do something that you like with passion, then no matter what you do, you'll be successful.

> —ANONYMOUS
> ST. PAUL, MINNESOTA
> YEARS RETIRED: 3

* * * * * * * *

PEOPLE WHO ARE NOT RETIRED THINK there is just nothing for the retired person to do at this point in their life. Well, forget that, folks! I have time to help many family members or neighbors who need that little extra aid for whatever reason. For me, it means caregiving for my aging parents; then there is taking care of the house, the car, pets, and sometimes, late at night, enjoying those moments called "leisure" for retirees!

> —L.H.
> SAN ANTONIO, TEXAS
> YEARS RETIRED: 1

* * * * * * * *

RIGHT AFTER I RETIRED FROM EDUCATION, I was lobbied to run for the school board, and I've been on it ever since—for a time as the president. A lot of people asked me to run for the city council, but I felt I knew a lot more about schools than about city government. This gives me a sense of purpose: I'm doing something for young people, who are the mainstay of our community.

> —J.L.
> CENTRALIA, WASHINGTON
> YEARS RETIRED: 9

A MAN, A PLAN

GIVE YOURSELF A FEW MONTHS AFTER retirement before you think about part-time work (if you have to think about it); plan fun activities for those first few months. As I worked on my finances, I came up with a plan that will let me be comfortable after 10 years of retirement. In the meantime, I will have to work part-time to enjoy the things I want to do. The plan is to think about combining my other interests with paying jobs. Among the considerations: working in a garden center during the heaviest season; working in a ski resort so that I can improve my skiing; becoming a "temp" so that I can experience a lot of new job situations and people; volunteering in national parks (room and board is free, but no salary); marketing my photos at crafts fairs or other venues.

—PHIL MACKALL
ARLINGTON, VIRGINIA
YEARS RETIRED: 1

I FIND THAT SO MANY PEOPLE, MYSELF INCLUDED, are forced to retire before they need to and before they want to, because corporations claim they're "rearranging" when really they're just getting rid of anyone over about 55. They'd much rather hire someone younger, who earns less and has fewer vacation days. I had worked for the same corporation for almost 20 years, and then one day I was just called into the office and told my job was ending. And my first response was, "What do you mean, ending?" All of a sudden, you're not part of the team anymore, and I've seen that happen to so many people before me and after me. I was really shocked and speechless, but I walked right down to the personnel office to find out about my severance package, and then I took my anger and resentment and turned them into fuel for finding another job, one that I enjoyed so much more. And the funny thing is, two weeks later, after I had been hired at my new job but was still finishing up at the old job, my boss called me and said they had decided they really did need someone to do my job and asked if I still wanted to work. And I said, "You bet I want to work, but not for you. I've already taken another job."

—VI HOWG
MINNETONKA, MINNESOTA
YEARS RETIRED: 5

AFTER 35 YEARS IN ADVERTISING, I was ready to retire, but I wanted to continue using my brain. I started writing some tips for seniors and retirees, and friends suggested that I send what I had written to a publisher. As a result, my reference guide for seniors and retirees, called *Invent Your Retirement: Resources for the Good Life,* was just published.

—ARTHUR KOFF
CHICAGO, ILLINOIS

* * * * * * * *

YOU HAVE TO LEARN TO SAY NO AND ONLY DO THE THINGS that you want and/or need to do. Retired people need to be assertive about finding activities within their abilities. Then they need to be generous with their skills and time, positive ... and no whining!

—ANONYMOUS
NEVADA
YEARS RETIRED: 13

* * * * * * * *

THOUGH I AM SOMEWHAT RETIRED PROFESSIONALLY (at least slowed down), I am not in a retirement mode emotionally or intellectually, and I have actually been giving seminars on helping people prepare for retirement. As a psychiatric social worker, I try to help people look inside themselves in order to explore and express their deepest interest. It is not always easy, but very gratifying.

—BEVERLY ZEIDENBERG
BETHESDA, MARYLAND
YEARS RETIRED: 2

A MEANINGLESS WORD

I DON'T BELIEVE IN THE WORD RETIRE. I've learned that once we stop having interests and helping people, we slowly die. It's so important for us to have something to get up for every morning. We have a choice of what we would like to do. If I had nothing else to do, I would go out and help people learn English and work with children on reading. There are so many things all of us can do. But if we aren't doing something that is meaningful, our life ceases.

—Mary Lou Cook
Santa Fe, New Mexico

BEST THING ABOUT RETIREMENT

WE HAVE TWO GRANDKIDS (8 AND 10), and we get to spend more time with them. Sometimes we keep the kids while my daughter is working. We have a lot of fun with them, especially at those ages. And I also do more things with my own kids than I did when I was working. For example, my daughter bought an old house, and I helped fix that up.

—CHALMERS GABLE
MARION, TEXAS
YEARS RETIRED: 5

* * * * * * * *

GETTING TO SLEEP THE HOURS YOU WANT TO SLEEP, and doing what you want to do, when you want to do it. That sounds kind of selfish, but when you work for 34 years and you have to be somewhere and on someone else's time, eat on their schedule, rush off to work, and then come home and constantly think about what you didn't get finished at work ... well, being on your own clock and not someone else's is just the best!

—HARRIET SMITH
SAN ANTONIO, TEXAS
YEARS RETIRED: 2

I WAS A BIOLOGY TEACHER AT OUR LOCAL HIGH SCHOOL. In retirement, I am a professional writer. I was always interested in writing, and I finally became so determined to be published that I submitted letters to the editor, contributed to my church newsletter and to anyone else who would accept my items!

—JoAnn
Joppa, Maryland
Years retired: 9

* * * * * * * *

IDLE HANDS

Retirees who go back to work part-time or decide to volunteer reportedly feel happier than those who stay at home.

* * * * * * * *

MY SCHOOL DISTRICT AUTOMATICALLY PUTS ITS RETIRED TEACHERS into "super sub" status. This means that for one day of substitute teaching, I make $140 as opposed to $80. If you're a retired teacher, subbing is the perfect part-time job because it pays well, it's flexible, and you get to keep in touch with old colleagues and friends.

—Kathy
Washington, D.C.
Years retired: 1

I DIDN'T REALLY WANT TO QUIT WORKING AFTER I RETIRED, but I didn't want to be in another demanding career. I wanted to do something completely different and also had to work around the disability of my blindness. Since I'm not able to drive, that restricted what I did tremendously. A business based in my home seemed ideal. My sister is a massage therapist, so I looked into that and found I enjoyed it.

—J.S.
SCOTCH PLAINS, NEW JERSEY
YEARS RETIRED: 4

* * * * * * * *

I WAS QUITE FOCUSED ON MY WORK. It was and still is difficult for me to realize that I am no longer in the mainstream of science. But I found something that is worthwhile to me. I'm the executive editor of a journal entitled *Progress in Lipid Research*. It is an international review journal. My job is to invite established scientists from around the world to write reviews on topics as they relate to the general field of lipids.

—HOWARD SPRECHER
COLUMBUS, OHIO
YEARS RETIRED: 5

* * * * * * * *

IN RETIREMENT, I'VE GOT A BUSINESS WITH MY HUSBAND. The work we're doing now is a blessing in our lives. Our joy is doing it together and going out on our little trips. Along the way, we go for a bike ride or go for a picnic. It gives me joy.

—ANONYMOUS
ST. PAUL, MINNESOTA

ASK NOT ...

BEFORE I RETIRED, I WORKED AT THE STATE CAPITOL in a job where I had to be strictly nonpartisan. But after I retired, I got back into politics, became a delegate, and went to the Democratic convention in Boston. I ran as an "Old Lady with a Young Mind," and I got elected on that platform. I was using a walker at the time, because I had just had my hip replaced, and my daughter made a sign to put on my walker that said, "I'm Old But I'm Not Greedy." That sign caused a lot of people to stop and talk to me and ask what it meant, and that led to some great discussions about Social Security and Medicare and taxes. I met a lot of people with that sign, and that's how I got elected. Politics is really a great place for retired people to put their energy. You can really make a difference.

—JANET
MINNEAPOLIS, MINNESOTA
YEARS RETIRED: 10

I SURVIVED RETIREMENT by opening my own computer business. It allowed me to meet new people and use my computer skills to help others. Otherwise, I would have been lonely sitting at home without a purpose to my days. It also meant I wasn't depending on my husband for petty cash. I believe women should always be self-reliant, even when retired.

—SUSAN FUSS
TORONTO, ONTARIO
YEARS RETIRED: 5

* * * * * * * *

I DIDN'T PLAN ON WORKING AGAIN FULL-TIME, but I'm back in the swing of things. I'm teaching psychology classes at a community college: six courses, 16 classes a week! I was working part-time, but the head of the psychology department got a promotion and asked me to take on extra classes for her. It's really interesting work.

—DONNA RICH
CHARLOTTE, NORTH CAROLINA
YEARS RETIRED: 4

* * * * * * * *

I HAVE A PART-TIME JOB AS A JUDGE for the Democratic Party. Basically, I'm a judge at a polling location at every election, local and national. I've been doing this for six years and enjoy it, although it's more like volunteering because the pay is minimal!

—M.A.R.
DURHAM, NORTH CAROLINA
YEARS RETIRED: 8

MY HUSBAND AND I DECIDED THAT since we suddenly had all this extra time on our hands, we were going to be productive and go into business together. It's not anything formal: In the summer, we mow our neighbors' lawns. In the winter, we shovel their snow. Each job brings us about $20, which is a great way to earn a little extra spending money while staying in shape and helping people who might not be able to per-form physical labor themselves.

—ELISABETH
ELYRIA, OHIO
YEARS RETIRED: 4

* * * * * * * *

TOO MUCH FREE TIME?

In 2003, the average retiree watched 43 hours of television a week.

* * * * * * * *

I'M A REALLY BIG BASEBALL FAN, and when I started easing out of my day job, I applied and was hired for a position as a concierge host for the Seattle Mariners. It's been a real delight. I get to meet people, see baseball games for free, and still get paid.

—HAROLD JAFFE
REDMOND, WASHINGTON
YEARS RETIRED: 2

OPPORTUNITY CALLING

I HAD BEEN A WRITER, JOURNALIST, and radio personality in earlier years. When I got to be over 60, I wasn't as interested in having a lot of work. I had other things I wanted to do: staying in shape, skiing, and building things. At one point, I had an idea to do oral histories for people for their families and for organizations. I started out recording my girlfriend's father, who was 94 at the time. I hadn't thought I would do it as a business, but it was so successful and so liked by the family, I thought maybe I'd do that for other people. Next, I did one for my ex-wife's family for her father. And that got universal acclaim. So I thought, "I'll start a little business." The idea is, at some point down the road, a great-grandchild who has never met his great-grandmother will want to know about her life. And it will be there on a CD, in the great-grandmother's words and in her own voice. I love doing this. I interviewed something like 10,000 people in my working life, but this is as much fun as I've ever had.

—MICHAEL CREEDMAN
SAN FRANCISCO, CALIFORNIA

I'M INVOLVED IN THE AARP TAX-AIDE PROGRAM, which provides tax preparation help to seniors and low-income people. I didn't have any particular experience in tax preparation— just doing my own—but I've always liked math and have a knack for it. Volunteers get five days of training, and then they can pick the site they'd like to work at. I work two afternoons a week, and we help about 30 people a day. When you get someone with a very low income, and you can get as much as $3,000 back for them, you just feel good.

—MARY ANNE PAGE
MINNEAPOLIS, MINNESOTA

* * * * * * * *

I ALWAYS TELL MY GIRLFRIENDS THAT IT'S OK for people our age to work, but they shouldn't be working at McDonald's. Nobody looks good in those uniforms, but especially not people of our age.

—ANN MARIE BUSH
POLAND, OHIO

* * * * * * * *

START A BUSINESS. I know that many start-up businesses fail, but I didn't have the income pressures that so many people do when they're just beginning a business. I was able to treat my new career as a hobby that got out of hand. I'm earning money now and my business is growing slowly, but I don't have to tear out my hair and starve in order to get it going.

—J.S.
SCOTCH PLAINS, NEW JERSEY
YEARS RETIRED: 4

MY WIFE AND I HAD BOTH BEEN IN EDUCATION, so it seemed natural we would go in that direction with our volunteer work. We set up a Dollars for Scholars program, providing educational opportunities for children. Since we started the program, we have raised more than a million dollars in scholarships for our community. Because my wife and I are such firm believers in education and it's been instilled in us, if we can help somebody else's child get an education, that gives us a nice, warm feeling. I started kindergarten back in the 1930s, and now in 2005, I'm still involved in education.

—B.L.
CENTRALIA, WASHINGTON
YEARS RETIRED: 13

* * * * * * * *

I LOVE TO SOLVE PROBLEMS, and I was always interested in computers. When I retired, I thought it would be fun to write software programs for network administrators, so I started my own business. It feels good to help solve problems. For example, computer users in school systems are constantly changing due to changes in enrollment. I created software that automatically removes students from the network when they leave school. It feels good to know that I've made someone's life easier. There's also a nice feeling that comes with success.

—JAMES EVANS
REPUBLIC, MISSOURI
YEARS RETIRED: 5

I'VE BEEN RETIRED FROM THE UTILITY COMPANY FIVE YEARS, but I've had my own classic car company on the side about 15 years. I started it on a lark and really got into it. It's kind of mushrooming and doing well, and now we're refurbishing classic cars and selling them around the world. It's just really fun, and I can make some money at it. And it's the kind of thing, if you want to devote more time to it, you can; if you want to devote less time to it, you can.

—CHALMERS GABLE
MARION, TEXAS
YEARS RETIRED: 5

* * * * * * * *

KEEPING BUSY

An AARP study showed that approximately 70 percent of baby boomers intend to work full- or part-time while they collect their pensions.

* * * * * * * *

RETIREMENT CAN BE A LOT LIKE FALLING OFF A CLIFF. One day you are fully occupied, and the next day you are wondering what to do. I think you have to retire slowly and gracefully. I still work part-time so I won't have to fall off a cliff.

—YITZ
MANCHESTER, UNITED KINGDOM
YEARS RETIRED: 8

MY PENSION AND SOCIAL SECURITY have been almost enough, but I am not one to feel secure without a little savings. I like to keep some extra money coming in somehow. This is a good idea for anyone looking to retire: to have a skill you can use once in a while to keep you busy, make you feel useful, help your bank account a little. I do some home nursing every now and then, stay with a new mother for a few days, that kind of thing. I have one friend who got a real estate license, and her husband got a broker's license, and she helps her friends and their children with real estate—not as a full-time thing, just every now and again. She enjoys it.

—BETTY
DURHAM, NORTH CAROLINA
YEARS RETIRED: 8

* * * * * * * *

I DON'T BELIEVE IN RETIREMENT. Retooling yourself is the idea.

—MICHAEL CREEDMAN
SAN FRANCISCO, CALIFORNIA

* * * * * * * *

I STAY ACTIVE WITH MY PART-TIME JOBS. And I tell my wife it's a good way to meet girls.

—JAMES SALTER
YOUNGSTOWN, OHIO

I WAS LOOKING FOR AN INVESTMENT that would bring in some extra money but not require a lot of time to run. I found a storage business for sale near our lake home. My wife and I agreed to buy it. It is very low maintenance. I have to mow it during the summer months, but that is about it. This is a growing area, so I don't have trouble finding renters. I get one or two who don't want to pay their rent, but overall everyone is good about mailing me their payments. It's the perfect business!

—J.L.
CLIMAX SPRINGS, MISSOURI
YEARS RETIRED: 10

* * * * * * * *

MY ADVICE FOR A SUCCESSFUL RETIREMENT CONSISTS of three essential things: First, stay intellectually active. Keep your mind working. It doesn't matter what you're working on; it needs to keep working. Second, remain physically active. I ride my bike to work—13 miles—as often as I can. It's a fair workout. And third, have future plans. I'm leaving in a week for the Philippines, and then I'm going to China to visit my daughter and her family. That's one of the essentials: not necessarily knowing what you'll do tomorrow, but having an idea that next year maybe I'm going to be doing this, and in three years I'll be doing that.

—ROBERT L. ZIMDAHL
FORT COLLINS, COLORADO
YEARS RETIRED: 1

IT'S NOT ABOUT THE MONEY

RETIRED PEOPLE ARE A HUGE LABOR FORCE in the volunteer world. If they're able, it's better for them to utilize their skills and interests. Everyone should contribute while he or she can. In doing so, you'll feel better about yourself and stay even healthier. Plus, the structure helps.

—DEB CARLSON KLAIN
CLEVELAND, OHIO

. . . .

IF YOU HAD TOLD ME HOW MUCH ENJOYMENT A PERSON could get out of doing something and not getting paid for it, I would not have believed you. I spent most of my life on the fast track, trying to advance career-wise and make as much money as I possibly could. If it didn't pay, I had no interest in it. But my wife has been involved in many organizations, and she guilted me into spending some time with her at our library. I fussed about it at first, but now I can't spend enough time there. I especially enjoy time in the children's area and watching the fun and excitement of the little ones as they pick out a book that they get to take home. I feel guilty, most days, because I get more out of it than I give.

—DAVID FELZKE
MORGANTOWN, WEST VIRGINIA
YEARS RETIRED: 5

WE WERE BUSIER WITH VOLUNTEER WORK after retirement than we were before. She did work with a food bank and Meals on Wheels, and I did work with Planned Parenthood, the school board, and the fire department.

—GEORGE RIES
SEATTLE, WASHINGTON
YEARS RETIRED: 30

• • • • • • • •

I DON'T BELIEVE YOU SHOULD PROFIT from our capitalist society and not give back to those who need it. After I retired, I joined an international program through my church that sent us to Ecuador to help with children and education there. It wasn't so much hands-on as it was using my business experience to set up systems that would help people. It was extremely rewarding. And it was a beautiful part of the world. Give back. You finally have the time to do it; just do it.

—E.R.
TAMPA, FLORIDA
YEARS RETIRED: 10

I'M 93 NOW, AND I RETIRED at the end of the academic year of 1982. But I still go to the university two to five days a week, doing things that they ask me to do. Sometimes they ask me to do something I don't want to do, and I say no. Remain active in things you like to do. That doesn't mean you have to do them all the time. Just enough to keep you occupied. And stay in close touch with people. The interaction with others is important. Even if they're always complaining, that's better than nothing!

—FRANCES LOMAS FELDMAN
PASADENA, CALIFORNIA
YEARS RETIRED: 24

* * * * * * * *

SINCE RETIRING, I'VE UNDERGONE a drastic values clarification. I didn't realize how much of my life had been spent "majoring in the minors" until I was no longer working. Now, I have a new sense of time and a realization that life isn't infinite. Consequently, before committing to any activity, I strongly consider if it's worth my time. For example, I love to volunteer. But I used to run around like a chicken with her head cut off, trying to attend every single volunteer meeting because I felt I should be there. Now, I skip most of the meetings but contribute 120 percent to individual projects I feel are worthwhile. Life is so much more meaningful now.

—GAY
DENVER, COLORADO

VOLUNTEERING IS WITHOUT A DOUBT my single favorite activity. I work with a variety of groups, doing publicity for one, serving on the board of another, helping organize an auction for another, and so on. The variety of activities and the opportunity to make lots of new acquaintances and friends is wonderful.

—SUSAN
TAYLOR, TEXAS
YEARS RETIRED: 3

* * * * * * * *

I GOT VERY INVOLVED WITH THE American Association of University Women, I joined the board of I Love a Parade, which helps homeless people to find work through the arts, and I regularly visit nursing homes with an elderly woman from church. I also serve on the environmental action team at church, I coordinate the art exhibits there, and I've been in charge of the rummage sale for the past three years. I enjoy the things I do, but I am trying to be careful to restrict myself to certain things and not take on others. I'm working very hard to create downtime.

—CYNTHIA
ST. PAUL, MINNESOTA
YEARS RETIRED: 8

I WORKED AS A NURSING ASSISTANT IN CRITICAL CARE, and it was stressful. I put my 10 years in and was eligible for retirement. Then I heard about a part-time program for seniors at The Bonne Bell Company, working on the production line. The people are my age, and we are not in competition with younger people. It helps to supplement my Social Security checks, but it also keeps me off the couch. I want to be active and still have something to contribute.

—FRANCES STETZ
CLEVELAND, OHIO

THE BIG 6-0

In the year 2006, as many as 8,000 baby boomers turn 60 years old every day. Tommy Lee Jones, Diane Keaton, Bill Clinton, Oprah Winfrey, and Donald Trump are among them.

YOU CAN'T JUST QUIT AND SIT IN A CHAIR NOW. You'd go nuts or eat bonbons and blow up and die or something. You have to do something. Don't isolate yourself!

—ALLAN S. ROSS
SAN ANTONIO, TEXAS
YEARS RETIRED: 1

IT'S NOT A GOOD IDEA TO RETIRE COLD TURKEY. I did, and at first I thought it was great not having to get up in the morning. I'd roll out of bed at 11 a.m. and spend the day leisurely browsing around Barnes & Noble. After about a month, the excitement wore off, and I began to miss the daily challenge and stress of my job. For that reason, I'm currently putting in an application for an assistant principalship. Some of us just weren't meant to stop working, I guess.

—JEFFREY WACO
NEW YORK, NEW YORK
YEARS RETIRED: 2

* * * * * * * *

I'M IN A SORT OF COMPROMISE WITH RETIREMENT: I'm almost 68, and I'm working at the library as a staff writer four days a week. This means I still have the satisfaction of work and more free time at the same time. It gives me the amazing gift of three-day weekends, which, after four years, is still a pure delight. By Friday evening, I sometimes think it's Saturday, and I still have a weekend. Then by Sunday evening, I'm ready to go back to work.

—SUE
PHILADELPHIA, PENNSYLVANIA
YEARS RETIRED: 1

* * * * * * * *

HAVE YOU NOTICED that all the synonyms for *retire* are depressing?

—ANONYMOUS
CALIFORNIA
YEARS RETIRED: 17

TO SOME, RETIREMENT MEANS THAT YOU STOP WORKING. But if you love what you're doing, retirement is more about finding ways to do the same thing on your own terms. The secret to retirement for me has been to find ways to keep teaching without having to get up every single morning at 4:50 a.m., and without having to go to work every single day. I love days off here and there, but my eyes cloud over when I don't have something to plan for.

> —JAMES MAHONEY
> YARDLEY, PENNSYLVANIA
> YEARS RETIRED: 8

* * * * * * * *

I'M A SEMIRETIRED FINANCIAL PLANNER. I do some consulting work for some of the bigger companies here in Youngstown. It's nice because I really don't have to answer to anyone, and I can set my own hours. I can pretty much pick and choose which projects I want to get involved with. I don't really need the money, but I wouldn't want to be fully retired. I guess I'm a type A personality, but I can't sit still long without work.

> —BERNICE ZLATOS
> YOUNGSTOWN, OHIO

* * * * * * * *

REMEMBER, YOU ARE A VALUABLE CITIZEN whether you work or not.

> —GEORGE RIES
> SEATTLE, WASHINGTON
> YEARS RETIRED: 30

RETIREMENT IS A RECENT MAN-MADE IDEA. It's not natural. You think the pioneers retired when they reached a certain age? It's just not the way things are supposed to be. We were made to work.

—GREG DEVRIES
POLAND, OHIO

* * * * * * * *

WHEN I RETIRED IN 1992, I started thinking about getting a part-time job. A friend who was a manager of a local credit union said, "We may have a job for you." So they hired me. My younger daughter couldn't believe it. She said, "Dad, you only have a three-day retirement?" It just seemed like the right thing, and so that's what I did. I kept working for them for eight years.

—B.L.
CENTRALIA, WASHINGTON
YEARS RETIRED: 13

* * * * * * * *

WORKING SINCE MY RETIREMENT HAS OPENED UP a whole new world to me that I knew virtually nothing about. I have been working as a part-time librarian, and it has been wonderful. My friend who works at the library suggested I give it a try, but I had no experience doing that kind of work. I've been learning as I go. I love it. I actually look forward to it each morning. If you are going to work after you retire, you might as well try something different.

—MITCH TERRIS
BOARDMAN, OHIO

AFTER A LIFE OF TEACHING, I thought I would retire and never want to set foot in a classroom again. But after a few years, I became friendly with some new neighbors and started tutoring their little girl. It was such a different experience than being a teacher; doing it because I wanted to help, rather than as a job, made it incredibly rewarding when that girl's math grade went from a C- to a B+. So I decided to tutor in the local school. The kids are so grateful.

—FRANK
CHARLESTON, SOUTH CAROLINA
YEARS RETIRED: 5

* * * * * * * *

THINK ABOUT DOING SOMETHING COMPLETELY DIFFERENT. My wife retired from the university and started a mediation business, which is what she had done in her career. But she's also starting an orchid business. She loves gardening and orchids and became good at growing and taking care of them. She said, "Let's try a little business thing and sell them." She likes it very much.

—EUGENE C. BIANCHI
ATHENS, GEORGIA
YEARS RETIRED: 5

* * * * * * * *

SITTING HOME, READING THE PAPER, and watching TV is great for about one week!

—ROY CLARY
BROOKLYN, NEW YORK
YEARS RETIRED: 1

Within Your Means: Money Tips

The number one piece of financial advice regarding retirement hasn't done you any good in years: "Start saving early." For that reason, we'll spare you the talk about how much money you should have put aside: The reality is that, regardless of how well you've planned, you now have a certain amount of money, and you probably know how to spend it. In case you need help, however, we asked retirees for money tips—among them, what to spend money on, and how they keep their finances organized.

KNOW AS MUCH AS POSSIBLE ABOUT YOUR ASSETS. My wife and I do everything ourselves. There are three benefits to doing this: First, you don't have to worry about anybody cheating you. Second, it keeps your brain alert. Third, it's cheaper!

—ANONYMOUS
CORVALLIS, OREGON
YEARS RETIRED: 11

* * * * * * * *

HIGHER STANDARDS

The number of people 65 years of age and over who live below the poverty level has decreased dramatically over the years, from 35 percent in 1959 to 10 percent in 2003.

* * * * * * * *

THE IRS WILL ALLOW YOU TO GIFT $10,000 a year, maybe more, to one person. I'm fortunate enough to have the money to do that for my three grandchildren. I give to them at Christmas, and as you can imagine, they look forward to it. One caveat: They have to put 25 percent into savings. The rest, they can do what they want. I find that most of the time they put it in investments or buy things for their home.

—E.R.
TAMPA, FLORIDA
YEARS RETIRED: 10

THE FIRST THING YOU SHOULD DO WHEN you're considering retiring is to go over your finances with a financial adviser or accountant. Make sure that you will have enough income to live the lifestyle you want before you make a move.

—JOHN R. BRIGHT
ALLENTOWN, PENNSYLVANIA
YEARS RETIRED: 10

* * * * * * * *

JOIN AARP AS SOON AS POSSIBLE. There are so many discounts that are available to you as a member. For instance, I just bought my son a Home Depot gift card for his birthday last week. When I presented my AARP card, they gave me a 5 percent discount, so I was able to get more money on the card than I probably would have spent otherwise. AARP is an organization that really understands the needs of its members, and they tailor the program to meet those needs.

—MARY CLAYTON
GREEN MOUNT, VIRGINIA
YEARS RETIRED: 7

* * * * * * * *

I LIKE TO SPEND MY MONEY ON CHARITABLE THINGS. I like going to plays and the theater. I've been a season-ticket subscriber to the USC football team and basketball team for 75 years. I signed up when I was a freshman, and I continue to go to the games.

—FRANCES LOMAS FELDMAN
PASADENA, CALIFORNIA
YEARS RETIRED: 24

THE MOST IMPORTANT THING I DID BEFORE RETIREMENT was pay off my condominium. I have no mortgage payment, which means that my housing costs are only the condo fee plus property taxes. I also was frugal, tracking my expenditures and cutting back in creative ways. This enabled me to retire with sufficient savings to travel and have adventures. I know how to live solely on my pension. I am spending my first year trying to figure out what I can do when I grow up!

——DALE SUSAN BROWN
WASHINGTON, D.C.

* * * * * * * *

YOU ARE ALLOWED TO USE THE MONEY you're saving in an IRA to pay for certain expenses that your kids might be running up. But if the grandkids need money, they should talk to their parents.

——PEGGY WEHR
WOODWORTH, OHIO
YEARS RETIRED: 7

* * * * * * * *

I SPEND MOST MONEY IN TRAVELING. I give money to charities. It makes me feel fine. I enjoy music, and I spend money on going to symphonies. I enjoy spending money on restaurants. I'm not a high spender, but I like having conversation and wine and good food.

——EUGENE C. BIANCHI
ATHENS, GEORGIA
YEARS RETIRED: 5

PREPARE FOR IT AHEAD OF TIME. Use your vacations to try out retirement ideas. Visit communities you think you might like to live in. Meet happily retired people, find out how they put their lives together in new ways, and learn from them. I took a sabbatical in my 50s and rode my bike in New Zealand, England, and Ireland and led bike tours for Vermont Cycling. I loved the tours so much I knew that I had to do more of them in retirement. My sabbatical helped me figure out things I wanted to do and didn't want to do in retirement. It also influenced me to retire while I was young enough to do these ambitious things (60) and to save every penny so I could have enough money to do them.

—EMILY KIMBALL
RICHMOND, VIRGINIA

PLAN AHEAD 2

It's important to have a solid financial plan in place before you retire. Start with these simple steps:
- Set a date for your retirement.
- Estimate how many years you will need retirement income (yes, this means thinking about your life expectancy).
- Calculate the amount of retirement income you will receive.
- Develop a yearly budget.

MY WIFE WOULD SAY MY FAVORITE WAY to spend money is to not spend it. That said, a good way to spend money is to spend it on someone else. I give a lot of money annually to local organizations like the food bank in my county. That's much more appealing to me than buying clothing. And I spend my money on my children. I'm inclined to give them books; I don't know whether they read them or not. And this past Christmas, I gave them each a goat! They didn't actually receive the goat; there's a program called Heifer International whereby you can give money to buy a goat for people in a developing country. I bought goats in my children's names. The children liked that.

—ROBERT L. ZIMDAHL
FORT COLLINS, COLORADO
YEARS RETIRED: 1

* * * * * * * *

WHEN I FIRST RETIRED, I SPENT ABOUT $60,000 IN ONE YEAR on a bunch of frivolous crap I didn't need, including boat equipment and a new car. The combination of extra free time and an "I've worked so hard all these years; why should I deny myself now?" attitude can be very damaging to your bank account. Before retiring, make certain you understand the difference between a "want" and a "need."

—JEFFREY WACO
NEW YORK, NEW YORK
YEARS RETIRED: 2

IT WAS IMPORTANT TO BE FINANCIALLY INDEPENDENT when I retired. I didn't want to worry about working. I didn't want to worry if my hobby made an income. For instance, photography is something I'm interested in, and if income comes from it, fine; but that's only in the back of my head. If it doesn't, then it continues as my hobby.

> —GARY SMITH
> SAN ANTONIO, TEXAS
> YEARS RETIRED: 1

* * * * * * * *

UNCLE SAM

Social Security provides the largest share of income for older people.

* * * * * * * *

WHEN WE STARTED TO PLAN FOR RETIREMENT, my husband and I sat down with a financial planner to see what our situation looked like. It's a good idea to have an expert look at your assets and financial situation objectively. Another good idea is to update your wills and create directives. No one wants to do these things, but they are important. It eases the burden, and you can then focus on just enjoying yourselves.

> —LOUISE WARNER
> NEW PHILADELPHIA, OHIO
> YEARS RETIRED: 5

YOU CAN'T LIVE ON SOCIAL SECURITY. It's like $16,000 a year, and you really can't enjoy yourself, or even do a lot of things you're used to, for $16,000. Late in my working life, I had tried to make different investments in stocks and bonds. In the end, it turned out to be a good thing.

—SONYA
BROOKLYN, NEW YORK
YEARS RETIRED: 10

* * * * * * * *

MY WIFE ENDED UP BEING HOSPITALIZED for several months, and I didn't know where I was going to get the money to pay the bills. I found out that you can take money out of your IRA early to pay for some of that stuff without penalty. It saved me a lot of hand-wringing trying to figure out where I was going to get the money.

—DENNIS RUSSO
WOODWORTH, OHIO
YEARS RETIRED: 4

* * * * * * * *

ABOUT SIX MONTHS BEFORE I RETIRED, I knew I was going to be in the market soon for a new car. I decided to buy it while I was still working instead of waiting until I was officially retired. It's much easier to get financing for a major purchase like a car while you can still list an employer on the application. It always looks good to have a job when you are trying to borrow money.

—SHANNON LIETWILER
KEEZLETOWN, VIRGINIA
YEARS RETIRED: 1

IT'S NEVER TOO LATE

MY COMPANY SET A POLICY OF OFFICIALLY PREPARING retirees five years before retirement. The special retirement seminar was not offered before that. Partially because of that, I assumed that five years was enough time. It was not! I was lucky; I will still be OK because, late in the game, I met with a financial planner. The planner helped me to analyze my real situation and to develop a workable plan. My first meeting was about a year before retirement. The biggest change I had to make was revising the way I viewed a mortgage. I had hoped to pay off my house shortly after I retired, but I could not afford the rate on the retirement payments I would be receiving. They helped me see that changing to a 30-year mortgage and not worrying about paying it off was the best option for me because of the current financial and personal picture. When I refinanced, I also included some mad money to help me with a few "last hurrah" items and a couple of house improvements.

—PHIL MACKALL
ARLINGTON, VIRGINIA
YEARS RETIRED: 1

IF YOU ARE ABOUT TO RETIRE, PLAN AHEAD. Plan ahead. Plan ahead. Pay off all monthly recurring bills. Have a complete physical, visual, and dental exam before you lose your standard health insurance. (That also includes minor outpatient gastrointestinal screening tests that should be done at about the age of retirement.) Insurance plans cost a lot more after retirement and often do not cover a yearly physical exam. Select and utilize the skills of a financial adviser who is knowledgeable in your area. Consider refinancing your house; I found a far lower interest rate. Think about making or updating your will. Consider investing in a long-term care policy and update your life insurance policy.

—L.H.
SAN ANTONIO, TEXAS
YEARS RETIRED: 1

* * * * * * * *

NEVER GO INTO RETIREMENT WITH DEBT. I made sure that I had everything, including my mortgage, paid off before I retired. This cut the amount of money I needed to live off by at least half.

—ANONYMOUS
LOS ANGELES, CALIFORNIA
YEARS RETIRED: 10

* * * * * * * *

I DIDN'T HAVE ENOUGH MONEY before I retired, and I still don't!

—DEWEY M. THORNTON
DURHAM, NORTH CAROLINA
YEARS RETIRED: 14

I NEED MORE MONEY TO LIVE ON NOW than I did when I was working. It has forced me to budget differently than I would have imagined. For instance, I have much more free time to shop, so I tend to buy more items impulsively, like shoes, than I would have while I was working, for the simple reason that I didn't have so much time to shop. Also, I spend more time in my apartment, so I tend to eat more snack food. It's not that I'm hungry, just that I'm home more so I eat more. To counter that spending, I eat out less than I did when I was working because I don't have co-workers to go out to lunch with. And now I don't have to buy clothes for work.

—BETTY SMITH
PITTSBURGH, PENNSYLVANIA
YEARS RETIRED: 5

STATES THAT TAX SOCIAL SECURITY BENEFITS

Colorado	New Mexico
Connecticut	North Dakota
Iowa	Rhode Island
Kansas	Utah
Minnesota	Vermont
Missouri	West Virginia
Montana	Wisconsin
Nebraska	

DARK THOUGHTS

I GUESS IT'S NEVER TOO EARLY TO PLAN for your eventual demise; I'm told it's inevitable. My financial planner insisted I create a will right after my retirement was official. It seemed morbid to me and like something only an "old" person would do. But he told me that people of any age can make one and that if you have any real property you really should have one. He said that without it, you can't be sure what will happen to your assets after your death, and that in certain situations the government can even claim some of it. Well, that was all I needed to hear. I'd rather throw my stuff away than give it to the government. Get yourself a will.

—EDNA STENZEL
VIENNA, OHIO
YEARS RETIRED: 2

. . . .

BE SURE TO LET YOUR FAMILY KNOW EXACTLY what your wishes are regarding your remains and your funeral. There is no such thing as being too specific; anything left unsaid will be decided by someone else. Even if you are alive, you may be incapacitated and unable to convey your wishes. Do it while you are still able.

—R.M.
BOARDMAN, OHIO
YEARS RETIRED: 2

MY KID INSISTED THAT I BUY A PLOT (really just a drawer) in a mausoleum. It's about 15 minutes from our home. You actually get to pick out your location within the building. Some cost more than others depending on size and location. I wasn't too keen on the idea at first, but I started warming up to it. Now at least I know, without a doubt, where my body will end up. And it should be paid off ahead of time so that it won't be a financial burden to my family. I guess the best thing is that it's inside, away from all the creepy crawlies in the ground. And I can visit my plot now and leave myself some nice flowers in case no one does when I'm gone.

—GEORGE RAPSO
GIRARD, OHIO
YEARS RETIRED: 1

PLAN AHEAD SO YOU CAN BE FLEXIBLE. My wife and I both found out within a week of each other that our companies were downsizing, and we were both eligible for a buyout package. It wasn't something that we'd expected or planned on. I know in my case, I thought I'd probably be working another couple of years. I was surprised to hear about it, but when I heard the buyout details, I became pleasantly surprised. We had to go back and think about it, figuring out whether it would work financially, but since we both had a buyout, which partially made up for the loss of income, it made the decision a lot easier.

—ANONYMOUS
WOODBURY, MINNESOTA
YEARS RETIRED: 9

* * * * * * * *

THE LONGER I LIVE, THE LESS I SAVE MONEY, and the more of my saved money I spend on my family. You know what they say: You can't take it with you. I think you should spend the money on your family while you can, instead of willing it to them once you're gone. This way you can share in the fun.

—AGNES DAVIDSON
WILLIAMSTOWN, KENTUCKY
YEARS RETIRED: 1

* * * * * * * *

MY RETIREMENT FEAR WAS, "Would the money stretch?" Budgeting is the key. Set a budget on paper and stick to it.

—C.R.
SAN ANTONIO, TEXAS
YEARS RETIRED: 1

YOU MOST LIKELY HAVE VERY CONSERVATIVE INVESTMENTS that pay next to no interest. Our daughter came to us and needed a large chunk of money to renovate a house. She guaranteed us a rate of return that was modest, but still more than the next-to-nothing interest we were earning in our safe accounts. Now, I would only recommend this if you absolutely know your kids are trustworthy—and even then we wrote up official documents just in case—but in our case it worked out wonderfully for all parties. My daughter got the money cheaper than from a bank (and let's face it, the bank didn't want to loan her that much anyway), and we got all of our money back with better interest than we were earning.

—MARY C.
TUCSON, ARIZONA

* * * * * * * *

TO DEAL WITH YOUR HMO, get a doctor who is really good at writing letters. My husband's oncologist saved us over $8,000 on medications this way.

—DONA
NEW YORK, NEW YORK

* * * * * * * *

MONEY SHOULD BE SPENT ON THINGS YOU WANT TO DO. If you play golf and do it passionately, spend your money there. Every human being has a chance to do something that makes him happy.

—RICHARD BING, M.D.
PASADENA, CALIFORNIA
YEARS RETIRED: 3

WE HAVE A RULE THAT ANY MONEY we make after retirement is our own to spend as we like. Neither of us is accountable to the other. Our income from Social Security, investments, and pensions is joint money, whose spending we decide together.

—JOSEPH EMIL VUCINOVICH
REDMOND, WASHINGTON
YEARS RETIRED: 7

* * * * * * * *

IT'S HARD TO TELL HOW MUCH MONEY YOU'LL NEED TO RETIRE. It's like making a bet on how long you'll live, which is a little spooky. It's also been hard to let go of the part of me that wants to make money. I've spent so much of my life thinking about making money, to just let that go is not in my nature. I appease myself with eBay. I find things at thrift stores and estate sales and sell them on eBay. It's not much money, hardly any, really, but it appeases the breadwinner in me.

—R.R.
CHARLESTON, WEST VIRGINIA
YEARS RETIRED: 1

* * * * * * * *

GET YOUR COST-OF-LIVING ESTIMATES and then double them. We thought we'd worked out everything about the cost of retirement. We went through all of our bills for 10 years, we got a new roof and a new car, our house was paid for. But everything goes up over time, and your income doesn't.

—ANONYMOUS
PETALUMA, CALIFORNIA
YEARS RETIRED: 13

"Honey, I'm Home!": Dealing With Domestic Changes

For years, you've been spending at least eight hours of every workday away from home, dealing with deadlines and virtual strangers. Now, you're spending almost all your waking hours in the same place that you slept, and the person you deal with most is someone you know all too well. It's not an understatement to say that there's an adjustment period with retirement. Here's how others dealt with the challenges of getting to know their spouse all over again, and what it felt like to discover their new, retired identity.

RETIREMENT IS A BIG ADJUSTMENT. You can't work at a job for 40-some years, and one Monday just not go in to work! Make sure you will have enough things to keep you busy. I had a hard time adjusting and almost made my wife crazy because I didn't do nearly enough. But over time I've come up with routines and things to do to fill my days.

—JOHN R. BRIGHT
ALLENTOWN, PENNSYLVANIA
YEARS RETIRED: 10

* * * * * * * *

I SPEND A FAIR BIT OF TIME IN MY STUDY, writing, while my wife does a lot of charity work in a thrift shop. Consequently, we don't follow each other around all day wondering what to do next, which I think would have led to friction.

—B.L.
SAN JOSE, CALIFORNIA
YEARS RETIRED: 8

* * * * * * * *

BEING TOGETHER 24/7 AFTER YEARS and years of his being gone all day or traveling a lot was the biggest challenge. Continue your life as you did before retirement occurred, but set some time to be together: reading time in the afternoon, cocktail time before dinner.

—NOLA SMITH
TAMPA, FLORIDA
YEARS RETIRED: 25

WHEN I FINALLY RETIRED, IT WAS DIFFICULT FOR BOTH OF US in the beginning. Since he had retired first, he came and went on his own. After I retired, I found myself questioning where he was going, what time he would be back, and so on. And if I sat down to do the crossword puzzle in the newspaper in the morning, he would ask me if I was "going to do anything" that day. That irritated me. It was my time to retire, and if I wanted to do the crossword puzzle, that was up to me! It took a while to adjust to being together so much of the time. I had to reinforce that the kitchen was my territory and I was the boss there. Often, he would come into the kitchen and ask what I was doing, why was I doing it that way, and so on. After a while, I would go down to his shop in the basement and ask what he was doing and why he was doing it that way! He soon got the message.

—LINDA DIBERNARDO
PORTSMOUTH, NEW HAMPSHIRE
YEARS RETIRED: 5

* * * * * * * *

IF YOU HAVE A GOOD MARRIAGE, it's just delightful being around each other 24/7. But then, Jim has never alphabetized my spices. That happened to a friend of mine. It did not work: That husband was escorted out of the kitchen.

—J.L.
MINNEAPOLIS, MINNESOTA
YEARS RETIRED: 10

I WAS AFRAID THAT WHEN MY WIFE and I were forced to spend so much more time together than we were used to, it would lead to a lot more fights. But we've gotten along splendidly. I guess I worry too much. It helps that she takes one night a week to see the girls and I do a guys' night out just about every Friday.

—BILL DAVIS
STRUTHERS, OHIO

* * * * * * * *

TOGETHERNESS

Research shows that married couples are happier if they retire at about the same time.

* * * * * * * *

WE DEFINITELY HAVE DIFFERENT STYLES. I like to get up and watch *The Today Show* while I drink coffee and look at the paper. Dick likes it quiet. So we have had to negotiate this a little. When Dick is around, I feel more like I have to be doing something productive. I think that is my problem, though, and not his. We have a big enough house that we don't really have to interact 24/7.

—HELENE
SALT LAKE CITY, UTAH
YEARS RETIRED: 2

MY WIFE WAS PANICKED. She was afraid that I would follow her around the house all day giving her ideas on how better to run the house. Her condition of my retirement was that I had to get an office or go to an office each morning. I would have breakfast, kiss her goodbye, and go to a small office in our town where I worked on volunteer projects, did some tutoring of high school students, or whatever. I sometimes spent an hour and went to play golf, or I might work all day.

—C. WILLIAM JONES
EASTON, MARYLAND

* * * * * * * *

KEEP THE CONNECTIONS YOU HAVE and make new connections as individuals and as a couple. We have "our" friends, she has "her" friends, and I have "my" friends. That's good.

—GARY SMITH
SAN ANTONIO, TEXAS
YEARS RETIRED: 1

* * * * * * * *

I BASICALLY TOOK OVER THE HOUSEWORK, so that when she came home there was nothing for her to do. Her job became easier because she knew that she didn't have to do the vacuuming and waste weekends on chores. There are no sexist roles here: Why can't I pick up a mop? Being retired, it's my time to take care of the fort.

—MICHAEL
SAYVILLE, NEW YORK
YEARS RETIRED: 1

I WAS NEVER A PERSON WHO ENJOYED BEING ALONE, so I welcomed the opportunity to spend more time with my spouse now that I was home every day. (And luckily she's a great cook and made me spectacular meals!)

—ANONYMOUS
TORONTO, ONTARIO
YEARS RETIRED: 10

* * * * * * * *

HUSBANDS CAN LEARN HOUSEHOLD CHORES, and wives can learn to do the business for the family. Remember, at some point, one of you will be doing all of it anyway. My wife had never had to even balance a checkbook. I took care of all business. On formally quitting daily work, I spent time showing her where various stocks and bonds were located and whom to contact, and explained our personal banking system, since we had several accounts. Sure enough, in the space of less than one year, I had two heart bypass operations. I was incapacitated. She had to take over all of our business and was able to do so.

—J.L.
DALLAS, TEXAS
YEARS RETIRED: 15

* * * * * * * *

I THOUGHT I'D MISS MY JOB A GREAT DEAL, but I didn't. From the first day I retired, I loved the freedom—especially on Monday mornings, when I could sleep!

—ANONYMOUS
SAVOY, ILLINOIS
YEARS RETIRED: 17

WOMEN WHO WERE STAY-AT-HOME MOMS need to be prepared for major changes when their husbands retire. My husband always wanted to know what I was doing. He wanted to organize my day, and then reorganize it. The trick is to not tell him your plans!

—MARY BRIGHT
ALLENTOWN, PENNSYLVANIA
YEARS RETIRED: 10

* * * * * * * *

DOMESTIC BLISS

Now that you're free from the daily grind of going to work, why not free yourself from those household chores as well? For those who can afford it, in-home services are available for everything from housecleaning and yard work, to grocery shopping and cooking.

* * * * * * * *

RETIREMENT IS GREAT, BUT WHEN you've spent 30 or 40 years only seeing your spouse a few hours a day, being together all of the time can take some adjusting. I started playing golf a couple of days a week; it works out well for both of us.

—JIM EYRE
JACKSONVILLE, TEXAS
YEARS RETIRED: 6

WHEN MY HUSBAND AND I RETIRED, we did everything together: golfed, played bridge, and so on. Never once did we get sick of each other. If you enjoy the activity in addition to the company, that really helps!

—B.A.R.
BAYONET POINT, FLORIDA
YEARS RETIRED: 25

* * * * * * * *

OUR DECISION AT THE POINT OF RETIREMENT was that I wouldn't be with my husband 24/7, and we have kept to that. In terms of friends and activities, we have "yours," "mine," and "ours." That has worked perfectly. We usually have breakfast together and discuss plans for the day and menus. And we come back together at dinnertime, unless we have a joint activity planned in the middle of the day.

—F.M.
ERDENHEIM, PENNSYLVANIA
YEARS RETIRED: 14

* * * * * * * *

IT'S IMPORTANT FOR RETIRED COUPLES to have a little time away from each other occasionally. I like to go away for the weekend with my sisters. And I really don't want Bill to go to the grocery store with me and rush me. It's my own time. When I'm shopping, I want him to be out fishing or at home reading. You have to respect each other's space.

—BARBARA STEVENS
GATLINBURG, TENNESSEE
YEARS RETIRED: 6

GOING INTO BUSINESS TOGETHER is the best possible practice for retirement you could have. My husband and I worked together for nine years as a real estate team, so spending too much time together after retirement won't be an issue for us.

—BRENDA JUSTICE
WICHITA, KANSAS
YEARS RETIRED: 1

* * * * * * *

IT'S VERY DIFFERENT TO BE TOGETHER 24 HOURS A DAY, seven days a week. She plays golf and loves gardening. I have a workbench in the garage and study multiple subjects that I'm curious about. But when we're both in the house, we have to learn how to respect each other. My wife and I listen to different radio stations; she likes talk radio and I prefer music. We listen with headphones if we are in the same room and want to have it on.

—FRANK HAWK
LAKELAND, FLORIDA
YEARS RETIRED: 3

* * * * * * *

I THOUGHT THAT WAS THE IDEA OF RETIRING; to spend more time with my wife. If you can't enjoy being together after spending a lifetime earning the right to do so, maybe you shouldn't have been married in the first place. I couldn't wait to spend more time with my wife. I feel bad for anyone who feels differently.

—DALE JENNINGS
FROSTBURG, MARYLAND
YEARS RETIRED: 2

TIPS FROM A RETIRED EXECUTIVE

AMAZINGLY, HOUSEWIVES SPEND A LOT OF TIME out of the house. And while she is engaged with shopping, groceries, shopping, laundry/cleaning, shopping, and other errands, with careful planning you can have the whole house to yourself! However, it's best for both of you if you keep an "office," either an executive suite with a cubicle and steno-copier service, or stake out a corner at Starbucks or Barnes & Noble. Remember, she took you "for life," but not for lunch every day.

A good idea is to plan a meeting for lunch with her on a regular basis. It will be fun to do it, and both of you can avoid any feelings of guilt or abandonment. If you really want to be a hero, I suggest you plan, buy for, and prepare the evening meal once a week. The fact is, she is sick of second-guessing your tastes and figuring out what to do each day, and since you are retired, she doesn't have that "break" of a business dinner every once in a while, when she can just make a TV dinner for herself.

—T.S.
TAMPA, FLORIDA
YEARS RETIRED: 12

MAKE SURE YOU HAVE HUMAN INTERACTION EVERY DAY. I remember when I had children and I was in the house away from work, it was hard. Retirement is similar, especially if you're not married. I was very lucky when I retired; my grandson was starting university in my town, and he actually lived with me for a while. I still see him a lot. But mainly I see friends. I make sure there's a reason to get up and shower.

—G.H.
CHAPEL HILL, NORTH CAROLINA
YEARS RETIRED: 2

. . . .

HAVING TO ADJUST TO YOUR SPOUSE is something many retirees may not expect. Sure, you've lived with them all these years, but through the years, they change; they aren't the same person you married. In fact, you've both changed, and you come home and find out you're both so different than you thought you were. You've got to have time to yourself; you've got to have freedom.

—DEE EYRE
JACKSONVILLE, TEXAS
YEARS RETIRED: 6

. . . .

IT HELPS IF YOU HAVE A BIG HOUSE. We enjoy spending time together, but we have three floors in our house, which gives us lots of room to escape.

—ANONYMOUS
ANACORTES, WASHINGTON
YEARS RETIRED: 10

IT WAS A PLEASURE TO WAKE UP WHEN I wanted to and to think, "What do I want to do today?" It was my day. Right after I retired, people would ask me, "Well, what are you doing?" I thought I had to come up with something. But I would say, "Nothing but what I want to do." And that's the truth!

—H.I.H.
DURHAM, NORTH CAROLINA
YEARS RETIRED: 7

* * * * * * * *

COMMUNICATION IS KEY

Married couples should sit down and discuss a plan for life after retirement that includes finances, household roles and, especially, how much time they plan to spend together.

* * * * * * * *

I STILL HAVE A 16-YEAR-OLD KID AROUND THE HOUSE, and my wife works full-time, so I've assumed a lot of the domestic things: cooking, food shopping, getting my kid to school, going to soccer games. I don't do windows and don't do housecleaning. Anyway, I like cooking and food shopping more than my wife does. It's been pretty easy.

—M.R.
SAN FRANCISCO, CALIFORNIA
YEARS RETIRED: 1

I DON'T MISS WORK AS MUCH AS I THOUGHT I WOULD. I was
a practicing nurse for nearly 40 years, and it became such a
large and integral part of my life. I thought I'd have to find a
new identity. But after about a month of retirement, I found
that I didn't really need to work to find fulfillment in my life.
I've found just as much contentment by spending time with
my family and friends.

—J.E.
MORGANTOWN, WEST VIRGINIA
YEARS RETIRED: 2

* * * * * * * *

RETIREMENT REALLY TOOK SOME GETTING USED TO. It was the
first time in my adult life that I didn't have to think about
going back to work after a vacation. For a while it just didn't
feel right. To tell you the truth, I almost felt guilty about
being home while other men my age were still going off to
work each day. I found that the adjustment just takes time.
You can't rush yourself to feeling comfortable with it. It will
come in time. I just kept telling myself that I had worked hard
my whole life, and I deserved a break. A permanent one.

—REGGIE BONFIELD
FROSTBURG, MARYLAND
YEARS RETIRED: 5

* * * * * * * *

SOME PEOPLE GET LOST IN RETIREMENT because they don't
have structure. To avoid that, make sure you have a schedule.

—L.C.
STRATFORD, CONNECTICUT
YEARS RETIRED: 2

CLOSE ENCOUNTERS: LOVE IN THE THIRD AGE

ONE OF THE BEST THINGS ABOUT RETIREMENT is that it leaves you plenty of time to focus on the "fine points" of romance that sometimes get neglected when you're bogged down with work. My husband and I make sure to hold hands, sit close to each other, and make eye contact across a crowded room. He takes care of me when I'm sick, gets me a glass of wine, or goes to the store to buy me popcorn. We always say "please" and "thank you" and avoid criticizing each other. After 48 years together, our relationship is better than ever!

—GAY
DENVER, COLORADO

. . . .

PEOPLE ON THE VERGE OF RETIREMENT will be pleasantly surprised to find that once you retire and you both have unlimited time for each other again, you will quickly and easily fall into those old habits of trying to please each other again. If you never fell out of love in the first place, then it has always been there anyway. It's more often the lack of time that keeps you from realizing it. My advice is to just be there and spend time with each other. Enjoy the time you have together.

—J.E.
MORGANTOWN, WEST VIRGINIA
YEARS RETIRED: 2

IF YOU ARE LUCKY ENOUGH TO FALL IN LOVE at this point
in your life, don't play around. You don't have the time to
waste like you once did. Tell her how you feel. I met my
second wife on May 13. We were married three months
later, in August.

—M.K.
GREEN MOUNT, VIRGINIA

. . . .

IT WAS HARD TO RETIRE BECAUSE AFTER MY DIVORCE, about
halfway through my career, my work was really my life.
But slowly I realized that I had been using my work to hide
from the world. There were really very few social opportunities at work. Many of the women were younger than me,
and there was no room for romance in my life. Soon after
I retired, I joined a book club, which is where I met my
husband. He has brought me so much happiness,
and I'm so glad that I decided to stop working
and explore life a little, even if I was scared and
didn't know where it would take me. I guess I
can thank my arthritis for something!

—BETTY
DURHAM, NORTH CAROLINA
YEARS RETIRED: 8

DATING OLDER MEN CAN BE REALLY HARD. For example, the ordinary retired guy wants a woman to be really good-looking and physically to be in really great shape. But most men my age don't take care of themselves the way they expect women to. I give most of them a pretty low grade. And most men just want to stay home and watch TV, or they want to come over to my house and watch TV. But for most older women today, the whole world is exciting. We don't want to take care of some boring old man. For example, this older man called me, and we went out one time, and he's called several times since, and then he was mad because I hadn't called back, and finally I just told him, "Look, figure it out. I've been divorced since 1973—do you really think I want a relationship? I have my family, my job, and I need time for myself." I'm independent and I like it that way.

—ANONYMOUS
SEATTLE, WASHINGTON
YEARS RETIRED: 5

I WAS 38 AND HAD NEVER BEEN MARRIED. I wasn't even seeing anybody at the time, but my 87-year-old grandfather, who had been recently widowed, was. One time I was talking with him on the phone, and he started giving me advice about where to meet women (by the pool), how to "woo" them (hold hands), and how "fast" to go (after a few weeks, it was OK to go for a kiss). Now, it may not have been so relevant to dating in my generation, but I remember thinking I shouldn't pooh-pooh his advice, because "Grandpa is getting lucky, and I'm not!"

—M.S.
NEW YORK, NEW YORK

. . . .

NOTHING WILL REVIVE YOUR SEX LIFE like being home all day, every day, with your spouse. It's like the period right after you first get married all over again.

—CARL COOKE
CUMBERLAND, MARYLAND
YEARS RETIRED: 1

SOMEONE ONCE SAID HAVING YOUR HUSBAND retire is like having twice as much husband and half as much money.

—SUSAN
TAYLOR, TEXAS
YEARS RETIRED: 3

* * * * * * * *

THE FIRST 30 DAYS OF RETIREMENT, you're on a vacation. The next 30 days, you're starting to get uncomfortable. You're twitching, trying to find something to do, like paint dresser drawers. The next 30 days, you find something to do, like taking a class or playing golf, something that amuses you. And finally, the next month, you think, "What would I do if I could do anything?" And, of course, you can do anything, so you go out and go for it.

—FRANK HAWK
LAKELAND, FLORIDA
YEARS RETIRED: 3

* * * * * * * *

IF I START TO GET ON HER NERVES, I just go for a walk.

—TERRY HARRINGTON
CUMBERLAND, MARYLAND
YEARS RETIRED: 2

* * * * * * * *

I BOWL WEDNESDAY NIGHTS and she bowls on Thursdays. We could bowl together, but this way we get a little break.

—WALT BULLOCK
BARRELVILLE, MARYLAND
YEARS RETIRED: 2

I WAS LOOKING FORWARD TO RETIREMENT until it actually happened. There was a sudden realization that I was entering a new phase of life. I was bored those first few weeks. That phase only lasted a short time, though. I slowly started doing projects around the house that I had been putting off. I also started exploring new things. I had always wanted to go off-roading in Colorado. I finally bought a Jeep and went. I can't imagine working now. All of my friends have gone through a similar phase. You just have to give it some time. Think of life as an adventure, and you will never run out of things to do.

—J.L.
CLIMAX SPRINGS, MISSOURI
YEARS RETIRED: 10

* * * * * * * *

IT'S FUNNY HOW A JOB DEFINES WHO YOU ARE to a lot of people. So when you retire, you need to define yourself in ways other than your job.

—KATIE
MINNEAPOLIS, MINNESOTA
YEARS RETIRED: 2

* * * * * * * *

I HAVE THE GREATEST HUSBAND IN THE WORLD, but too much time together can drive you crazy. At some point in your day, take quiet time alone. You need your own space.

—MOLLY KOLB
JACKSONVILLE, TEXAS
YEARS RETIRED: 10

YOU'LL FIGURE OUT SOMETHING TO DO with your time. And if you don't, then your wife will find something for you.

—BARNEY WISTROM
LaVALE, MARYLAND
YEARS RETIRED: 6

. . . .

THE BIGGEST CHANGE SINCE I RETIRED IS THAT I get up later in the morning, and I spend time visiting with my wife, which we never did when we worked.

—JOSEPH EMIL VUCINOVICH
REDMOND, WASHINGTON
YEARS RETIRED: 7

New Horizons: Settling Into a New Place

There's something about retirement that taps into our nomadic sensibilities. Free people from the ties that bind, and suddenly they dream of living in a place they've never been. Or they make plans to go to a warm-weather destination like Florida. As a retiree in modern times, you have more options than any generation before you. The trouble is deciding where to go: Do you really want to sell the house you've lived in for so many years? Do you want to be near your kids and grandkids? Or do you want to be as far away from human contact as possible? Big city or retirement community? Read on for ideas about your next move.

IT WAS VERY EASY TO LEAVE THE CITY WHEN we retired and get away from all the cars and people. We looked for places on the beach in southern and northern California, and we finally settled on Bodega Bay. We still see our friends often, even though we don't live as near. We go there, or they come here.

—J.D.
BODEGA BAY, CALIFORNIA
YEARS RETIRED: 5

. . . .

IF YOU'RE GOING TO START GETTING OLD, the city is a good place to do it. Everything is here. Especially since I really haven't been driving so much now, it's so convenient. You can see a lot of things, even if you don't have a friend to do it with. You can go to a museum or do a show on your own, whenever you want. That's the life for me.

—SONYA
BROOKLYN, NEW YORK
YEARS RETIRED: 10

. . . .

WE STAYED IN OUR HOME FOR A FEW REASONS. First, it's paid for! Second, everything we need is within walking distance: the grocery store, drugstore, Kmart, fast-food chains, and restaurants. Third, we're on the bus route, so if the time comes that we can no longer drive, we can take the bus.

—MARY BRIGHT
ALLENTOWN, PENNSYLVANIA
YEARS RETIRED: 10

SOME OF THESE NEW RETIREMENT VILLAGES are like summer camp for older folks. We visited some friends who lived in one where we were considering moving, and on any given day, there were half a dozen classes or activities. And not just the usual golf, tennis, and bridge. They offered yoga, painting, woodworking, stained glass, and all sorts of oddball classes. It was mind-boggling!

—BONNIE DULFON
WALTHAM, MASSACHUSETTS
YEARS RETIRED: 3

* * * * * * * *

JOIN THE CLUB

Florida, Pennsylvania, and West Virginia are the states with the highest populations of people age 65 and older.

* * * * * * * *

DON'T SELL. REAL ESTATE ONLY INCREASES IN VALUE. The only way I would consider selling is if I were moving out of the area, but my kids all live around here, so I'm not going anywhere. Some of my friends have asked me why I don't sell and move into a condo or an apartment, but none of my kids has ever broached the subject with me.

—BILLY TRAMPER
FROSTBURG, MARYLAND
YEARS RETIRED: 1

WHEN I DECIDED TO MOVE OUT OF MY HOUSE and into a smaller apartment, I was careful to choose one that was within walking distance to places I would need to go on a regular basis, like a grocery store and a pharmacy. It's really important for people like me who don't drive. You don't want to have to call friends or family every time you need to get a roll of toilet paper.

—ALICE DUKE
COVINGTON, KENTUCKY
YEARS RETIRED: 4

* * * * * * * *

PEACE OF MIND

A study of census data shows that retirees living in big cities are moving to smaller towns that offer less congestion, lower crime rates and cheaper housing.

* * * * * * * *

I THINK YOU SHOULD SELL YOUR HOUSE. Having a house just isn't necessary once the kids are gone. I think people hang on to them out of fear that they'll die wherever they move, fear that they'll regret it as soon as it's sold. But I just don't see the advantage of hanging on to a big house.

—BETTY ZAYCHICK
CUMBERLAND, MARYLAND
YEARS RETIRED: 10

I'M NOT GOING TO SPEND THE LAST PART OF MY LIFE as one of these typical retirees living in Florida. It's too clichéd, and there are too many jokes to be made at your expense. There are plenty of other places in the country that you can go. Try living where I do, in Virginia's Shenandoah Valley. It is spectacular. There are so many outdoor activities to keep you busy that you'll feel as young as you ever have. And we have nowhere near the heat and humidity that they do in south Florida.

—MARIE LONG
HARRISONBURG, VIRGINIA
YEARS RETIRED: 2

* * * * * * * *

I WOULD NOT LIVE IN A RETIREMENT HOME. I'm 65, and I would have no desire to do that. My mother-in-law is 95, and even she's fighting going into a retirement home.

—ANTHONY TAFEL
CHRISTIANA, PENNSYLVANIA
YEARS RETIRED: 14

* * * * * * * *

I'M A REAL PACK RAT AND FOUND DOWNSIZING VERY HARD. We wore out two shredders, shredding every check we had saved over the years. In the end, we were burning them in our barbecue.

—ANONYMOUS
PETALUMA, CALIFORNIA
YEARS RETIRED: 13

DOWNSIZING YOUR LIFE

THE FIRST THING TO GO IS CLOTHING. A wardrobe for the working life doesn't fit retirement. Get rid of it! Somebody can use those clothes better than you. Next, work on getting rid of your "things." It's amazing what you have collected over the years. Think whether the children want them, but in general, pitch them! We got a storage place and put things in it until we were ready to admit we never would use them again, then we pitched them! You really don't need to keep all those sleeping bags, backpacks, books, 12-inch LPs, or the 8-track player.

—T.S.
TAMPA, FLORIDA
YEARS RETIRED: 12

JUST BECAUSE I'M RETIRING FROM WORK doesn't mean everything about my life is changing. I have my own home, and I plan on staying there as long as possible. I don't want to move to a special community, or a condo, or another state. Some people find that living in the same house (which hopefully is paid off) provides a crucial element of stability during what might otherwise be a period of unrest.

—ANONYMOUS
BALTIMORE, MARYLAND
YEARS RETIRED: 13

* * * * * * * *

WE RETIRED AND MOVED AWAY FROM THE TOWN that we had called home for more than 20 years. We went back several times that first year. Eventually, most of our friends also retired and were out traveling. We've since made new friends in our new town. We only go back to our old hometown for special events. It took us a year or two to make the transition, but we were much happier once we did. We started looking forward instead of looking back at what we had left behind.

—C.L.
CLIMAX SPRINGS, MISSOURI
YEARS RETIRED: 5

* * * * * * * *

ONE THING YOU NEED TO CONSIDER when moving somewhere to retire is how good the city's health care system is. It's more of a concern when you're older.

—BOB RICH
CHARLOTTE, NORTH CAROLINA
YEARS RETIRED: 5

IF YOU HAVE THE MEANS, BUY A CONDO ON A BEACH. We have one in northwestern Florida. Not a beach house; a condo. It's roomy enough for a few families to stay there, so we use it to visit and vacation with our kids and grandkids. But when we're not there, we don't have to worry about upkeep. We can have someone with the building check on it and fix any problems. With a beach house, we'd have more room, but we'd be on our own with the upkeep. That's not something you want to worry about in retirement.

—E.R.
TAMPA, FLORIDA
YEARS RETIRED: 10

THERE IS A SENIOR HOUSING HIGH-RISE IN MY TOWN that is extremely hard to get into. They put you on a waiting list until an apartment opens up. I just got the call last year, and I absolutely love the place. The morbid part is that you know nobody is moving out of there willingly. They are only leaving when they die. I guess one person's loss is another person's gain. If there is one of these kinds of places in your town, you should check it out. It sure beats a nursing home.

—BETSY ANDERSEN
CANFIELD, OHIO

PICK A PLACE TO SETTLE BASED on the activities it offers.

—B.A.R.
BAYONET POINT, FLORIDA
YEARS RETIRED: 25

IF YOU'RE MOVING, WAIT TO BUY A HOUSE, even if you think you know the area. We sold our home in Ohio and decided to live in Charlotte for a year before buying a house. It's the best way to really get to know a new area. When we found ours, we loved it right away. The housing development has a sports complex, a huge pool, book clubs and gourmet food clubs, and even an empty-nesters group. We went to an empty-nesters dance last night.

—DONNA RICH
CHARLOTTE, NORTH CAROLINA
YEARS RETIRED: 4

* * * * * * * *

NO PLACE LIKE HOME

The majority of retirees prefer to remain in the homes they have always lived in, rather than moving somewhere else.

* * * * * * * *

MY SISTER AND I ARE GETTING TO BOND NOW. I'm going to be moving into a new house near her, and until I can get in there, she's taken me in for a few months. We've never lived under the same roof since who knows when! So far, so good.

—J.L.
JACKSON, NEW JERSEY
YEARS RETIRED: 2

MY WIFE AND I LIVE IN A BIG OLD HOUSE where we raised our four daughters. We have lived there for 38 years. I love that house, but I think it's time to sell it. It's just so hard for my wife to keep up with the cleaning and for me to do all the upkeep. But my wife is adamant that we stay. She says that house is our home and we should stay there until we die. I understand her point of view, but I'm afraid that if we have to keep doing all this work ourselves, it's going to kill one of us. I got her to agree to have a girl come in once a week to help with some of the real tough stuff—like the floors and windows. It's tough on us financially, but it was tougher to get my wife to go along with it. It's the best compromise I could get.

—TODD COOPER
YOUNGSTOWN, OHIO

ALTERNATIVE HOUSING

- Retirement communities offer independent living with optional meals, activities, and housecleaning services.
- Assisted living arrangements provide housing and additional services for those who require limited assistance with personal care.
- Nursing homes offer housing and nursing assistance to those who are temporarily ill or in need of long-term health care.

I THINK IT'S BETTER TO GET RID OF TOO LITTLE before you move and then have to get rid of it later than to get rid of too much and be sorry something is gone. I'm really sorry about some things I got rid of. We had this deli slicer that we didn't use all the time, but we used it whenever all the kids came over and we made a roast. We got rid of it before we moved; now, I'm just sorry I don't have it anymore. We also got rid of all of our lamps, not realizing that the development where we moved wasn't really big on putting overhead lights into the rooms.

—ANONYMOUS
PETALUMA, CALIFORNIA
YEARS RETIRED: 13

* * * * * * * *

DON'T STAY IN YOUR HOMETOWN. Move about three or four hours away from your kids. That way, you can see them on holidays, birthdays, and during emergencies, but you're not constantly in their hair.

—GARY D. GALLAGHER
WILLIAMSON, WEST VIRGINIA
YEARS RETIRED: 1

* * * * * * * *

ONE OF MY DREAMS WAS THAT I would get a couple of boat oars and walk until someone asked me what the oars on my shoulders were for, and that's where I would settle. But we ended up moving back to where my wife grew up.

—MENDELL PETER SPARKS
SPRINGFIELD, MISSOURI
YEARS RETIRED: 15

MY HUSBAND WANTS TO SELL OUR HOUSE and live full-time out of our motor home so we can travel. I'm not so keen on this. I'd like to travel, too, but I also want to take up new hobbies, like painting. I know if I'm constantly on the road, seeing different things, I'll never maintain enough concentration to have any hobbies. Rather than fight about it, we decided to go the old-fashioned route and compromise: My husband said that if I get our house clean enough to live in, we'll stay. Everybody wins when you bargain.

—ELISABETH
ELYRIA, OHIO
YEARS RETIRED: 4

. . . .

I WORKED MY WHOLE LIFE TO AFFORD A BIGGER HOUSE; why would I sell it just because it's mostly empty? It's still mine. It's the most valuable thing I ever bought, and I'm not giving it up. One of my kids will get it when I'm gone. And I like the idea of at least some of my grandkids being raised in the same home where I raised my kids. If you have trouble keeping up with the cleaning, hire a maid. Or let it get messy. Who cares?

—J.L.
WOODLAND, MARYLAND
YEARS RETIRED: 4

On the Road Again: Traveling When There's No Rush to Return

When you're not thinking of where to settle next, you're probably thinking of your next great adventure. While there's always a cruise to take you to interesting destinations, many retirees get creative when it comes to travel. We asked people to tell us some of the best trips they've taken. Read on for tips on where to go and how to get there.

THE COAST OF MAINE, THE GLACIERS IN ALASKA, the historic buildings in Boston, the hills of San Francisco, the active volcano in Hawaii: These are all new entries in my memory bank since retiring.

—JANE HULMAN
BETHESDA, MARYLAND
YEARS RETIRED: 11

* * * * * * * *

DON'T JUST SIT AT HOME. My husband pointed out recently that we were free to go wherever we wanted or to live wherever we wanted. Our retirement checks are going to come no matter where we are. That's a nice feeling—not being tied to a place, a job, or a daily responsibility.

—SUSAN
TAYLOR, TEXAS
YEARS RETIRED: 3

* * * * * * * *

ONE OF THE BEST TRIPS WE EVER TOOK SINCE we retired was a bike tour of Italy. We biked from Pisa to Venice. Everything about it was great: the food, the hotels, the sights, the people. We didn't want it to end. And it was pretty easy, about 20 to 40 miles a day. There was one hard day when we climbed the Apennines, and it was 100 degrees and there were trucks spewing blue smoke. But then we got to the top and drank wine for two hours, and then it was downhill and shady on the other side.

—JIMBO
MINNEAPOLIS, MINNESOTA
YEARS RETIRED: 14

I'VE BEEN IN CONTACT WITH MY OLD COLLEGE FRIENDS.
About 12 of us lived together on the same floor in a dorm in college, and we had a ball. I hadn't seen some of them in 20 years, and yet when we got together at the beach, we picked up right where we left off. When you're retired, you need to make plans like that with old friends. We're all getting together again this summer, and I can't wait.

—H.I.H.
DURHAM, NORTH CAROLINA
YEARS RETIRED: 7

* * * * * * * *

GET A HUGE MAP OF THE UNITED STATES. Put it up on the wall. Put on a blindfold. Get a dart. Throw the dart at the map, and make your destination the place where the dart lands. It's great to plan a trip to somewhere you've never been and would otherwise never go. You can find fun and adventure anywhere you go. The first time I did it, we ended up going to Fowler, Kansas. It was a great little town that I would have never, ever seen otherwise.

—BENNY TADFORD
YOUNGSTOWN, OHIO
YEARS RETIRED: 3

* * * * * * * *

RETIREMENT IS IDEAL FOR DAY TRIPS: the beach, amusement parks (without kids!), or antiquing in nearby villages.

—T.S.
TAMPA, FLORIDA
YEARS RETIRED: 12

WHEN MY HUSBAND AND I WERE WORKING, we always felt we should spend our vacation time together. We continued to take vacations together for the first few years after we retired. Then it dawned on us: I didn't care to go off-roading in Colorado, and he didn't care to go gambling in Las Vegas. We were ruining the other one's good time. A couple of years ago, we started taking separate vacations. My husband goes to Colorado with his brother. I go to Vegas with my daughter or friends. We both come home happy. We're together all the time, so it's good to get away. We miss each other until we get back.

—C.L.
CLIMAX SPRINGS, MISSOURI
YEARS RETIRED: 5

* * * * * * * *

COMMERCIAL CRUISE LINES ARE NOT OUR STYLE: I'm not interested in sailing around the world in a horizontal Hyatt hotel. On a cruise ship, the average age is 63. But Semester at Sea is filled with people who are young; the average age is probably 22. The Semester at Sea is literally a trip around the world in a horizontal dormitory filled with people with raging hormones, none of which are mine. But it's a great way to see 10 different countries. If you are interested in seeing the world aboard a ship and can tolerate living 100 days with people who are much younger than you, give it a go.

—ROBERT L. ZIMDAHL
FORT COLLINS, COLORADO
YEARS RETIRED: 1

I LOVE TRAVELING ON GROUP BUS TOURS run by companies like AAA. They are fun and a great way to meet people and see new places. And it's much more cost-effective than going alone. I recently went to Gatlinburg, Tennessee, and I met people on the trip who I know will be lifelong friends. To me, the biggest benefit is that I don't have to do the driving: Amen to that.

—ROSEANN DICOLA
HARRISONBURG, VIRGINIA
YEARS RETIRED: 3

* * * * * * * *

KID-FRIENDLY

National parks are great for traveling with grandchildren. Park rangers offer educational programs that help build an appreciation for history, nature, and wildlife.

* * * * * * * *

ONE OF THE BEST THINGS ABOUT BEING RETIRED is the freedom to travel when I want. When my son and daughter-in-law asked me to stay at their house for a week to house-sit while they were away on vacation, there was no question; I had the freedom to do it.

—HELEN REICH
DUBOIS, PENNSYLVANIA
YEARS RETIRED: 5

WE HAVE BEEN TRAVELING NOW FOR SIX YEARS, and we have bought nine RVs! We've been to Arkansas, and we fly-fish in the Ozark Mountains, where the people are really friendly and hospitable. We go to Missouri, Iowa, Nebraska, South Dakota, and Wyoming, and we typically spend a month in Montana. On our way back, we've gone to Idaho, Utah, California, Nevada, New Mexico, Arizona, Texas, Louisiana, Mississippi, Alabama, and North Carolina. It's wonderful to meet new people and see new places and just be together.

—BILL CHARLES
BRISTOL, TENNESSEE
YEARS RETIRED: 6

* * * * * * * *

WE WENT ON A TWO-WEEK STUDY TRIP TO NICARAGUA, sponsored by a local college, to help people understand the sort of challenges that developing countries face, like environmental problems and issues of sustainable development. It was a great trip. And now, three people are coming from one of the agricultural cooperatives where we stayed, and we'll host them. I should be practicing my Spanish!

—KATIE
MINNEAPOLIS, MINNESOTA
YEARS RETIRED: 2

* * * * * * * *

CRUISES ARE ONE OF THE NEATEST WAYS to travel and also one of the best ways to meet new friends.

—DEE EYRE
JACKSONVILLE, TEXAS
YEARS RETIRED: 6

OUR MOST FUN ROAD TRIPS HAVE BEEN in our Roadtrek camper van. It's not a big unit, but we have everything we need: beds, a small kitchen, and a bathroom. It's our favorite way to travel. We can camp in a rustic state forest, in a private campground with nice shower and bath facilities, or in the middle of a city, like we did in Anchorage. It's like a modern covered wagon. And what's fun about a Roadtrek is that you see a lot of other people traveling in them, and you both roll down your windows and wave like crazy, because you know how much fun the others are having.

—ANONYMOUS
WOODBURY, MINNESOTA
YEARS RETIRED: 9

RESOURCES FOR TRAVELING ABROAD

- The U.S. Department of State (http://travel.state.gov) has all the information you need on passports and visas, as well as travel warnings.
- Travelvaccines.com will help you prepare yourself health-wise for overseas travel.
- AARP Passport offers travel discounts to members, as well as up-to-date advisories on weather, airline strikes, and flight delays.

FIDO'S RETIRED, TOO

AVOID GETTING A NEW PET IN THE YEARS leading up to your retirement if you plan to travel a lot. And if you already have a pet, think seriously about what you will do with it while you are gone. I wanted to spend as much of my retirement traveling as I could. But what I didn't really think about was what I would do with my pet while I was gone. It's been a real problem. I don't have any relatives whom I'd be comfortable asking to keep the dog while I'm gone for long stretches. And leaving the dog at a kennel is not only expensive, but it's not really good for the dog. Each time I did that, he seemed to hold it against me.

—W.T.
HARRISONBURG, VIRGINIA
YEARS RETIRED: 1

YOU HAVE TO DO ALASKA; WE DID. It is perfect for the retired—unhurried, full of variety, and uncommonly beautiful and peaceful. Our favorite memory is a spontaneous overnight en route to another destination, when we found a little town with great food, accommodations, and entertainment, in the middle of nowhere!

—T.S.
TAMPA, FLORIDA
YEARS RETIRED: 12

* * * * * * * *

BUY YOURSELF AN RV AND SEE THE COUNTRY. There is so much out there to see, and I'm not talking about the Grand Canyon or Mount Rushmore. There are so many interesting sights and little towns across the country that you'd never have the time to see during your working life. The best way to do it is to just start driving with no destination in mind. Just see where the road takes you.

—DENISE LABATOS
YOUNGSTOWN, OHIO
YEARS RETIRED: 3

* * * * * * * *

SEVERAL TIMES I JOINED A TOUR GROUP and took a chance on whether I'd like it and whether the people in the group would talk to me or not. I've always come back having made friends who remain my friends afterward.

—FRANCES LOMAS FELDMAN
PASADENA, CALIFORNIA
YEARS RETIRED: 24

WHEN YOU'RE WORKING, a vacation home is a real adventure, like a minivacation. But when you're retired, it's totally different. It's not nearly as pleasurable. Anticipation of a vacation is probably as much of the enjoyment as the travel itself. You won't feel the need for that vacation home quite as much as you did before.

—L.C.
STRATFORD, CONNECTICUT
YEARS RETIRED: 2

* * * * * * * *

A TIMESHARE IS NOT ONLY A GOOD INVESTMENT; it's a good adventure. We own a couple of timeshares—in Park City, Utah, and in Palm Desert, California—which allow us to travel to those places, and we also trade them. By trading our timeshares, we've traveled to Block Island, Rhode Island; Hilton Head, South Carolina; Italy; Austria; France. We've been to 10 or 12 different places.

—ROBERT L. ZIMDAHL
FORT COLLINS, COLORADO
YEARS RETIRED: 1

* * * * * * * *

IT GETS AWFUL LONELY ON THE ROAD. I missed being around my kids. They never tell you that in those travel brochures. Make sure if you are going to travel that you take someone along; even a dog will probably do.

—CHAD MORTON
POLAND, OHIO

WE HAVE A TIMESHARE DEAL THAT WE can use throughout the country. We just came back from three weeks in Southern California, where we stayed in timeshares in Anaheim and Oceanside, and we've stayed in several in Florida. Timeshares are great because you get a larger, nicer place to stay. If you're going to spend a week or 10 days in a hotel room, it's not real nice. But with a timeshare, you have a kitchen, a bathroom, a nice living area.

> —ANONYMOUS
> WOODBURY, MINNESOTA
> YEARS RETIRED: 9

* * * * * * * *

ONE OF THE BEST TRIPS I'VE TAKEN since I retired was to Australia. I went with a friend, and we were gone for six weeks. We arranged the trip so we would connect up a couple times with a group, but we also were able to travel on our own. We really liked that combined kind of trip. It was very expensive, but if you're spending that much money to go to Australia, you want to make good on the time.

> —M.L.
> BLOOMINGTON, MINNESOTA
> YEARS RETIRED: 15

* * * * * * * *

WHEN YOU'RE TRAVELING IN AN RV, with 250 square feet, you really have to respect each other's privacy.

> —BILL CHARLES
> BRISTOL, TENNESSEE
> YEARS RETIRED: 6

RETIREMENT IS PAYBACK TIME! It's now time for *me!*

—M.K.
SOUTHPORT, CONNECTICUT
YEARS RETIRED: 12

. . . .

YOU ARE NOT AS YOUNG AS YOU USED TO BE, and you have to plan your vacations accordingly. My wife and I went to Maui and hiked to the summit of a dormant volcano. Once you are up there, you can hike down into the crater. There is a sign that tells you to allow twice as much time for coming out as going in because of the thin air up there at 10,000 feet. I ignored the sign and paid the price: We had to keep stopping so I could catch my breath.

—COLIN McDOUGLE
CANFIELD, OHIO
YEARS RETIRED: 2

. . . .

I ORGANIZE GROUPS OF MY FRIENDS TO TAKE impromptu trips. Some of my friends would tell you that these trips are some-times *too* impromptu. But I think it's more fun if you just pick up and go. It's the kind of thing you do less of when you get older. People my age are often set in their ways and have to plan for months to take a weekend trip. I think the spontane-ity of my trips is what makes them so enjoyable. Just picking up and going on the spur of the moment takes people back and makes them feel younger again.

—JANE TABACHKA
GREEN MOUNT, VIRGINIA
YEARS RETIRED: 3

WE SWAPPED OUR HOUSE WITH SOMEONE who lives in France, and we spent three weeks in Provence last September. We swapped with an apartment in New York and went to the theater. It has worked very well for us so far. You're in their house and they're in yours, so you take good care of it. Traveling this way leads to wonderful, richer experiences.

—MICHAEL CREEDMAN
SAN FRANCISCO, CALIFORNIA

* * * * * * * *

GO SOMEWHERE YOU ALWAYS DREAMED OF GOING. There are certain things in the United States you need to experience before you die; for me that was Mardi Gras. I was lucky enough to retire at a relatively young age, and I could go down to New Orleans and really enjoy myself. You'd be surprised at how many older couples go there. I had always wanted to go but never had a chance.

—V.C.
COALBURG, OHIO
YEARS RETIRED: 4

* * * * * * * *

WHEN WE TRAVEL, WE GO TO ELDERHOSTELS. We really like them, and I've always thought the housing was fine. You do have to be flexible; if you go to Costa Rica, they're going to feed you rice and beans.

—JANET
MINNEAPOLIS, MINNESOTA
YEARS RETIRED: 10

I'VE GONE TO ALL THE PLACES I WANTED to go at least once. If I were giving advice on where to travel, I'd say, stay right here in California. There is nothing that you find in other places that you won't find here. My interest in other countries is in seeing how other people live. I've been to every country in Africa except Angola. I've been to just about every country in South America. There are all kinds of adventures and people, and they're all different in each country.

—FRANCES LOMAS FELDMAN
PASADENA, CALIFORNIA
YEARS RETIRED: 24

* * * * * * *

SOME OF THE TRIPS WE TAKE ARE BASED AROUND MY HOBBY, marathon running. There are races all over the world, and when I was working it was hard to get away. But just recently we went to a big marathon in Ottawa. It's a beautiful city with culture, nightlife, and great architecture. And I never would have seen it if they didn't have this big marathon there. We got there on a Friday, I ran the race that weekend, and we stayed a couple of days extra to see the sights.

—AARON
ST. PETERSBURG, FLORIDA
YEARS RETIRED: 2

* * * * * * * *

WHEN THEY TALK ABOUT YOUR GOLDEN YEARS, this is what they're talking about.

—MARIO ONCEY
POLAND, OHIO

The Possible Dream: New Hobbies & Activities

What with starting your own business and/or volunteering, visiting with family, moving to a new place, traveling, and balancing your budget, who has time for a job? But what about all those things you wanted to do once you finally retire: the hobbies that you never managed to fit into your busy schedule, or the new adventures you dreamed of launching as soon as you cleared your calendar? From quilting and gardening, to cycling across the country and running marathons, the retirees we talked to found fresh new pleasures around every corner.

WHATEVER IT IS YOU COULDN'T DO when you were working, do it now. The older you get, the more you realize that the old adage is true: Life is short. When you're physically and mentally able to do what you want to do, do it. Don't have regrets later.

—CHALMERS GABLE
MARION, TEXAS
YEARS RETIRED: 5

* * * * * * * *

I STARTED RUNNING ABOUT 30 YEARS AGO. After I retired, I wanted to challenge myself. I ran my first marathon about eight months after I retired. Now I try to run five days a week. It's my opinion that nobody maintains fitness for rational reasons. I say that because to do it, you have to make yourself uncomfortable. You have to be motivated by something else. In my case, it's to be healthy and mentally fit. Running is what works for me.

—JAMES EVANS
REPUBLIC, MISSOURI
YEARS RETIRED: 5

* * * * * * * *

ONE OF MY FIELDS OF EXPERTISE IN CRIMINAL INVESTIGATION was composite art drawing. Also, over the years of writing police reports I discovered a love of putting words together. So, from the first day of retirement I began to write short stories and do my own illustrations.

—BILL STRAIN
KERRVILLE, TEXAS
YEARS RETIRED: 6

I WAS ALWAYS HANDY AND ALWAYS WANTED TO TRY SCULPT-ING, but I never felt like I had the time or the opportunity. It's been an amazing experience for me, and I've created some pieces that decorate our home. I've also continued to garden as a hobby. I've always had a garden, and I practically grew up on a farm, so this was important to me. My wife and I moved to an apartment complex, but the town has gardens that are leased for the summer. I grow veg-etables, and I'm generally there a few times a week.

—CHARLIE
HARTSDALE, NEW YORK
YEARS RETIRED: 14

* * * * * * * *

MAY WE SUGGEST...

Didn't have time for hobbies before you retired? Check out www.HobbyWorld.com for ideas on how to spend all that newly acquired free time.

* * * * * * * *

I STARTED VOLUNTEERING WITH KIDS, visiting nursing homes, and assisting people with their grocery shopping and cleaning. I've never been happier. Helping others is absolutely my niche. Find yours and run with it.

—ANONYMOUS
HERSHEY, PENNSYLVANIA
YEARS RETIRED: 35

QUILTING: A SLAM DUNK

I'M CRAZY ABOUT BASKETBALL, TRULY A NUT. I loved basketball back in high school, and then college was great for basketball, and now I love to watch the Timberwolves and the university teams on TV. But I've found I just hate the long commercials, so I started making baby quilts when they come on. I can now do the blanket stitch without looking, so I can do that during the games, but the rest of the work I do during the commercials. I've made at least 50 quilts during basketball games. Then I pile a bunch into a big basket and take them down to the homeless shelter, because there are always new babies who need quilts. It's very satisfying to know my quilts are out there, even though I don't see the people who've gotten them. And I love combining my two interests, basketball and quilting.

—JANET
MINNEAPOLIS, MINNESOTA
YEARS RETIRED: 10

THE YEAR BEFORE I RETIRED, I got involved in cycling. After I retired, I had much more time to devote to it, and now I cycle competitively with other retired seniors. It gives you a great workout, and it's lots of fun. The best thing, other than staying in shape, is all the wonderful friends I have made by doing it. If you can find something that keeps you active, healthy, happy, and stimulated, go for it.

—R.D.
KEEZLETOWN, VIRGINIA
YEARS RETIRED: 2

* * * * * * * *

DON'T WAIT UNTIL AFTER YOU RETIRE TO FIND A HOBBY. It's not that easy to find something that you want to spend a lot of time doing; it's trickier than it sounds. I have friends who like to golf, but when they retired, they found that they didn't want to do it every day. For me, it's gardening. I could spend all day puttering around out there, and most days I do.

—ANONYMOUS
EAST PALESTINE, OHIO
YEARS RETIRED: 4

* * * * * * * *

I BELONG TO THREE TENNIS LEAGUES, I play golf two times a week, I belong to a reader's theater group, I sing with a band, and last year I was in five plays. If you get hooked up with a senior center, there's no limit to the amount of things you can find to do.

—JANIS
CARY, NORTH CAROLINA
YEARS RETIRED: 8

EIGHT OR NINE YEARS AGO I scratched my head and said, "What am I going to do when I retire?" I'd always had an interest in painting, so I went ahead and started taking classes. I don't consider myself a painter or an artist, but I've had a couple of shows. I've sold a few pieces at a very modest price from time to time. I like to be creative. It's important to look forward and find meaning in this life of ours. Painting is a new challenge for me.

—ROY CLARY
BROOKLYN, NEW YORK
YEARS RETIRED: 1

* * * * * * * *

THE LAST THING YOU WANT TO DO IN RETIREMENT is to sit around the house working or reading. Get up and out in the fresh air, even if it is just to take walks or ride a bike. Exercise cleanses the mind and body. I exercise at the YMCA, and play golf and platform tennis.

—C. WILLIAM JONES
EASTON, MARYLAND

* * * * * * * *

PLAY BOCCE: There's much more skill involved in that game than horseshoes, which many of my friends play. And it just looks better. Probably the best part is that anybody watching you play probably has no idea of the rules, so they always think you're better than you are.

—MARK TOOMEY
BOARDMAN, OHIO

RETIREMENT TO-DOS

For years I have been talking about what I will do. I finally sat down and made a long list of things that have been floating around in my head. Some examples:

- Read a book from cover to cover without stopping for things like work and obligations (I have about 30 books waiting for me).
- Paint my house and fix the gutters.
- Organize some other gardeners and help out at the local school or with senior citizens who need help with their yards.
- Visit all the friends I have been promising to visit over the years.
- Go with a friend for a month or longer on a hiking/camping trip in Alaska.
- Start leading retiree outings with an outdoor group that I used to actively participate in.
- Do a house exchange with people from German- and French-speaking countries so that I can develop my skills in these languages.

The latest addition to the list is to volunteer at national parks. It's free. I found out about it while reading a murder mystery. The book mentioned an opportunity in the Dry Tortugas. I researched it on the Internet and found it was for real and just one of many volunteer opportunities provided by the National Park Service. I'm now excited about volunteering in a variety of parks across the nation.

—PHIL MACKALL
ARLINGTON, VIRGINIA
YEARS RETIRED: 1

I ENJOY READING: I never had time to do that when I was working and raising kids. I also enjoy going fishing. I even went to Cancún, Mexico, with my daughter. You can only clean the house and do the laundry so many times.

—C.L.
CLIMAX SPRINGS, MISSOURI
YEARS RETIRED: 5

* * * * * * * *

SOMETIMES I WONDER, when did I have time to work? My new job is taking my granddaughter to her figure skating lessons and competitions. On Wednesdays, I have yoga and schedule doctor appointments. I want to take a computer class and a philosophy course. And we're always having events like graduations, parties, and church activities. My life is very busy, but it is good. I can't see myself sitting at home watching TV!

—E.M.
EDGEWATER, NEW JERSEY
YEARS RETIRED: 3

* * * * * * * *

I'M ON THE BOARD OF THEATER ORGANIZATIONS IN TOWN. Being involved with arts organizations—the symphony, National Public Radio—gives us more outlets to meet people. That keeps you going.

—ALLAN S. ROSS
SAN ANTONIO, TEXAS
YEARS RETIRED: 1

I ALWAYS ENJOYED GOOD FILMS, and so I joined a film club. After doing that for a year or two, I decided that I could do it better. I started a film society that shows foreign and independent films. I convinced high-powered speakers to address my group, formed a board of directors, and found a suitable venue. We are going into our ninth year, have established nonprofit status, and are getting great reviews and excellent crowds. It could be called "making your dream come true." It has certainly given me an interest that will carry me well through my retirement years.

—BEVERLY ZEIDENBERG
BETHESDA, MARYLAND
YEARS RETIRED: 2

* * * * * * * *

TECHNOPHOBIC?

SeniorNet is a nonprofit organization dedicated to "bringing wisdom to the Information Age" by promoting the use of computers and technology among adults 50 and older.

* * * * * * * *

PLAN ACTIVITIES. It doesn't have to be a retirement community if that doesn't interest you, but join a writing group or a volunteer organization.

—GRACE
CHAPEL HILL, NORTH CAROLINA
YEARS RETIRED: 11

MAD HOT BALLROOM

MY FAVORITE ACTIVITY IS BALLROOM DANCING. The age range of people at the ballroom is from about 50 to 92. And it's mostly single people. What's so fun about it is that every dance is an event and everybody looks so nice: People wear silks and satins and have their hair all shiny, and it's just kind of a little scene. And a woman who puts forth the effort will certainly get the attention. I'm very willing to tell a man when he looks nice. Men love to be flattered; they love attention. You'll definitely become one of their favorite people. And ballroom dancing is a wonderful way to stay in shape, because when you're dancing, you're getting great exercise; but when you're not dancing, you're constantly thinking about staying in shape so you'll look nice when you go to the dance. It's a huge motivator.

—D.S.
CHICAGO, ILLINOIS
YEARS RETIRED: 5

IT'S A MYTH THAT RETIREMENT AUTOMATICALLY translates into "more free time." Maybe I have the chance to watch a little more TV with my husband, but that's it. If I'm not catching up on household chores or tending to our animals, I'm volunteering with the local schools or the Boy Scouts. Everything seems exciting when you don't *have* to do it.

> —ELISABETH
> ELYRIA, OHIO
> YEARS RETIRED: 4

. . . .

SCALE YOUR ABILITIES TO YOUR AMBITIONS. I ski. I really enjoy it. But my reflexes aren't quite as good as they used to be, and my skiing is not that great at all. I recently went skiing with some friends, and I felt tight. I decided I was going to give it up. But a friend convinced me to go back with him. It was good advice. Instead of going on the black diamonds, I now go on the easier runs, and I enjoy it.

> —MICHAEL CREEDMAN
> SAN FRANCISCO, CALIFORNIA

. . . .

WHAT FLOATS YOUR BOAT AND MAKES YOU HAPPY? Your children and your grandchildren can't be your main interests; you have to have something outside of them.

> —M.A.R.
> DURHAM, NORTH CAROLINA
> YEARS RETIRED: 8

IT'S EASIER FOR PEOPLE WITH HOBBIES TO RETIRE because hobbies give you something worthwhile to do with your time. It doesn't matter what those hobbies are. I quilt, I play mah-jongg, I do yard work, I entertain, I travel, I cook, and I read. All of these things help keep my mind active and provide an excuse for regular social interaction.

—KATHY
WASHINGTON, D.C.
YEARS RETIRED: 1

* * * * * * * *

GENEALOGY IS A GREAT ACTIVITY WHEN YOU'RE RETIRED. It had always been in the back of my mind, and I toyed with the idea when the kids were little, but I never did anything about it. But as you get older, you realize, "If I don't do this, no one else will." And it's your responsibility to find this information, to talk to the few older relatives you have left, and pass it along to future generations.

—ANONYMOUS
WOODBURY, MINNESOTA
YEARS RETIRED: 9

* * * * * * * *

PLAY BINGO. I ACTUALLY PLAYED QUITE A BIT WHILE I was working, too, but now I have the time to travel around and play bigger tournaments. You'd be surprised how much money you can win. And I do win because now I'm getting enough practice to be pretty damned good at it.

—J.M.
BOARDMAN, OHIO

MY WIFE HAS KEPT UP WITH PEOPLE we knew in high school. We now see them pretty regularly. I belong to the Yacht Club, the church, the English Speaking Union, and the Sons of Confederate Veterans. I think these give me a good social outlet. At my age, if they weren't worthwhile, I wouldn't bother with them.

—C.B.
JACKSONVILLE, FLORIDA
YEARS RETIRED: 23

* * * * * * * *

I STARTED TAKING PIANO LESSONS. We have a piano in our house, and at a certain point our kids said, "We're not taking piano lessons anymore." It was just sitting there; it was something I always wanted to try, so now I'm taking the lessons.

—M.R.
SAN FRANCISCO, CALIFORNIA
YEARS RETIRED: 1

* * * * * * * *

THE FIRST THING I BOUGHT FOR MYSELF after my retirement was the most expensive pair of walking shoes I could find, and I got walking. The best part of being retired is to get up at the crack of dawn and just walk before most people are out of bed. There is such a peace and serenity in the world at that time of day, and most people don't have a chance to see it while they are still dealing with careers.

—PATTY MELANGER
HARRISONBURG, VIRGINIA
YEARS RETIRED: 2

BACK TO SCHOOL

ONE OF THE DANGERS OF LIVING IN A retirement community is that you can come down with fuddy-duddyitis. It's essential to get out of the community and be around people of all ages. I take graduate-level classes with people my children's age and then language classes with people in their 20s. It's fascinating and intellectually challenging, not to mention interesting to hear how they talk, dress, walk. I'm going with some students to Spain this month to learn Spanish. It should be challenging since they are in their 20s and will be going 100 miles per hour, while I'll be doing 40 miles per hour!

—FRANK HAWK
LAKELAND, FLORIDA
YEARS RETIRED: 3

. . . .

I HAD ALWAYS WANTED TO LEARN MORE ABOUT CARS so that I could work on my own car, so I took some auto-shop courses. It's fun because there is no pressure, and you have all day to do your homework. Now I can save a few bucks by doing minor repairs myself instead of taking the car to the shop all the time.

—JOHN PACE
UNITY, OHIO
YEARS RETIRED: 4

RETIREMENT IS THE TIME TO FIND ANSWERS TO QUESTIONS.
I always wanted to know more about art history. Every
time I'd be watching a show or a movie and some reference to the Mona Lisa or Monet or some other painter
would come up, I'd wish I knew more about it. Now I'm
taking the time to learn all I can. And I can throw away
those little Post-it Notes in the back of my brain.

—MARCIA COULIS
BOARDMAN, OHIO
YEARS RETIRED: 1

* * * * * * * *

THEY OFFER ADULT-EDUCATION CLASSES on the lower west
side of Manhattan. I'm really enjoying it. It gets me out of
the house, it keeps me alert. If you just sit in the house,
you don't accomplish very much. We need tasks. We need
goals. It's great to have an outside school that can act as a
force and drive you. It gives your days structure.

—ROY CLARY
BROOKLYN, NEW YORK
YEARS RETIRED: 1

SO MANY COLLEGES AND UNIVERSITIES NOW OFFER accelerated degree programs that are perfect for retired people. The work is crammed into a shorter time period, but since you are not working anymore, you have plenty of time to do the work at home. I'm working on finishing my bachelor's degree in personnel management.

—BESSIE SARVER
BAZETTA, OHIO
YEARS RETIRED: 5

• • • • • • • •

WHEN I ACCEPTED EARLY RETIREMENT DUE TO LAYOFFS, my company offered a training/education allowance as part of the package. I told the company I was going to learn to be an aerial photographer, which meant I needed my pilot's license. So they paid for me to take flying lessons, and I got my license and did many solo flights. It fulfilled a lifelong dream of mine!

—JACK MORRIS
WALTHAM, MASSACHUSETTS
YEARS RETIRED: 16

WE TAKE A LOT OF CLASSES AT THE LIFELONG learning institute at the university. You pay just once a year, and then you can take as many classes as you want. I've taken classes in literature and bookmaking, and my husband has taken classes in jazz and reading the Bible. It's been said that one of the downsides of retirement is that you stop meeting people and making new friends, and with our classes, we keep on being challenged and we keep meeting new people.

—JEANNE
MINNEAPOLIS, MINNESOTA
YEARS RETIRED: 7

* * * * * * * * *

I HOPE THAT IN THIS DAY AND AGE RETIREES don't avoid taking classes because they are worried that they are too old. That's ridiculous and archaic thinking. Nowadays there is such diversity on college campuses that all age groups are represented, especially on the weekends and at night. I've found that even when I am one of the older ones in my classes, the kids aren't snickering about me. They often come to me for help. Please don't miss an opportunity to better yourself because of fear of rejection. Those days are gone.

—PAULA DONNEL
PATMOS, OHIO
YEARS RETIRED: 2

FIGURE OUT A WAY THAT YOUR HOBBY CAN HELP OTHERS. I like to knit, so I joined a group that meets two times a week to make sweaters and afghans. We then distribute our products to meaningful organizations across the nation, like Volunteers of America or veterans groups.

—ANONYMOUS
LOS ANGELES, CALIFORNIA
YEARS RETIRED: 10

* * * * * * * *

HOME-IMPROVEMENT PROJECTS are a good use of time. We recently bought our home, but it was in its original 1950s condition. We've had a lot of work done, but I decided to take on the painting. I painted a whole room in a single afternoon!

—ANONYMOUS
EL PASO, TEXAS
YEARS RETIRED: 2

* * * * * * * *

IN A LOT OF WAYS, YOU CAN STAY AS BUSY AS EVER, just with different things. After I joined the temple board, I found myself getting even more wrapped up in the local Jewish community than I expected. I'm also taking a class with our rabbi. No way would I have been able to get so involved if I were not retired.

—FRED
MILLER PLACE, NEW YORK
YEARS RETIRED: 2

NEED MORE IDEAS?

I FINALLY HAVE THE TIME to write bad novels.

> —B.L.
> SAN JOSE, CALIFORNIA
> YEARS RETIRED: 8

* * * * * * * *

I SWIM THREE TIMES A WEEK. I sing in a choir. I'm active in my church.

> —E.M.W.
> SPRINGFIELD, MISSOURI
> YEARS RETIRED: 12

* * * * * * * *

THE LIST OF THINGS I GET TO DO NOW is endless: ski, fish, golf, tend my bonsai, garden, fix things, read, hike …

> —RICHARD
> SALT LAKE CITY, UTAH
> YEARS RETIRED: 3

* * * * * * * *

I'M IN THREE BANDS. I've been playing the trumpet since high school. I love it!

> —BOB RICH
> CHARLOTTE, NORTH CAROLINA
> YEARS RETIRED: 4

I BELONG TO THE NATIONAL SKI PATROL and spend about four hours a week doing work for them. I'm on the board of a local patrol at Tahoe, where we have a home, and also on a regional patrol board.

—J.D.
BODEGA BAY, CALIFORNIA
YEARS RETIRED: 5

* * * * * * * *

HAVE SOMETHING SET UP THAT YOU HAVE TO DO, because retirement is something you have to wean yourself into. I taught school for so many years that I missed the children when I retired, so I tutored for a few years until I was ready to quit completely. It takes three to five years until you are ready to relax. Try new things and see what fits you and your lifestyle.

—MARGARET MCCOWN
JACKSONVILLE, TEXAS
YEARS RETIRED: 16

* * * * * * * *

WHEN YOU RETIRE, CHANGE YOUR SUBJECT OF INTEREST. I feel somewhat sorry for people who cannot let go of things they have done for their entire lives. Let go and change your interest and do things you have wanted to do all your life but didn't have time or courage to do.

—RICHARD BING, M.D.
PASADENA, CALIFORNIA
YEARS RETIRED: 3

GET UP IN THE MORNING AND DO NOT WATCH TV ALL DAY.
Find something that can make a contribution. I'm setting up
this Emeritus College at Emory University that focuses on
helping retired academics. There's a lot of excitement about
it for me. But it can be done any thousands of ways. You
might want to be a dispatcher for 9-1-1, or you might want
to do something artistic.

—EUGENE C. BIANCHI
ATHENS, GEORGIA
YEARS RETIRED: 5

* * * * * * * *

I FOUND TIME TO GET BACK to my passion: salsa dancing!

—DEE
OAK LAWN, ILLINOIS
YEARS RETIRED: 1

* * * * * * * *

I'VE TAKEN UP GARDENING. I'm going to start by growing
myself into a couch potato.

—TOM BURDOCK
POLAND, OHIO
YEARS RETIRED: 1

* * * * * * * *

IF YOU'VE GOT SOMETHING YOU'VE ALWAYS WANTED TO DO,
you better do it before you retire. After you retire, you won't
have time!

—DEWEY M. THORNTON
DURHAM, NORTH CAROLINA
YEARS RETIRED: 14

SLEEP LATE ONE WEEKDAY MORNING AND THINK, "Wow! What fun is this!"

—NOLA SMITH
TAMPA, FLORIDA
YEARS RETIRED: 25

* * * * * * * *

YOU DON'T RETIRE FROM SOMETHING; you retire *to* something.

—CHARLIE
HARTSDALE, NEW YORK
YEARS RETIRED: 14

* * * * * * * *

DON'T RUSH INTO NEW THINGS TOO QUICKLY. Relax and breathe deeply and see what comes bubbling up and has been hidden under the aura of business during your working years.

—EMILY KIMBALL
RICHMOND, VIRGINIA

* * * * * * * *

I SOLD MY HOUSE and bought a big RV. Now my hobby is finding a place to park the thing, or looking for a repair shop in Kearney, Nebraska.

—M.L.
WENATCHEE, WASHINGTON
YEARS RETIRED: 5

GET INVOLVED IN OTHER THINGS THAT YOU ENJOY!

After retiring, I got involved with my church, my grandchildren, and traveling. It wasn't long until I was asking myself, "When did I have time to work?"

—MARGARET MCCOWN
JACKSONVILLE, TEXAS
YEARS RETIRED: 16

* * * * * * * *

I WORK PART-TIME in commercial real estate. I just moved here, so now I'll need to get my broker's license. For me, work *is* my hobby.

—S.K.
SEATTLE, WASHINGTON

* * * * * * * *

TRY TO AVOID GETTING COMMITTED to too many things; days go by quickly. I got up today at 7 a.m., meditated, took my kid to school, and read the newspaper. Then I managed my stock portfolio, which takes about an hour a day. Before I knew it, it was almost the middle of the day. I started getting tense; the day was disappearing, and I still had things to do.

—M.R.
SAN FRANCISCO, CALIFORNIA
YEARS RETIRED: 1

I'M ON THE BOARD of the English Speaking Union and of the Chicago Symphony Ladies' Auxiliary, and I'm very involved in church activities. There are far more cultural events in the city than I can ever attend. I'm as busy as I want to be.

　　　—L.F.
　　　　CHICAGO, ILLINOIS

* * * * * * * *

MY ONLY HOBBY IS SLEEPING LATE, reading the entire newspaper, and then lying down for a midmorning nap. But other days I take it easy.

　　　—JORGEN PATSILEVAS
　　　　SALEM, OHIO
　　　　YEARS RETIRED: 2

Staying in Shape: Mind, Body & More

I t's an uphill race: As you get older, you have to work harder just to stay the same. Slack off, and you fall back. Retirement means you've got the time to take care of yourself, and far fewer excuses not to. And while you're keeping your muscles, bones, and joints fit, don't forget to exercise your brain. Studies have shown that learning new skills, solving puzzles—even switching hands while you brush your teeth—can help keep your neurons nimble. Need ideas for things to do? Our respondents have plenty to say on the subject.

PAY PARTICULAR ATTENTION TO YOUR HEALTH. Don't let health issues slide. If your doctor says, "Go get a colonoscopy," get it. If you have all the time and money in the world and you're not healthy, you don't have anything.

—CHALMERS GABLE
MARION, TEXAS
YEARS RETIRED: 5

. . . .

I LOVE WATER AEROBICS. I used to go with a really funky group of old people at the Y. I just loved that, because we had great music and a fun leader, and we were really an eclectic group.

—JANET
MINNEAPOLIS, MINNESOTA
YEARS RETIRED: 10

. . . .

NOTHING KEEPS YOU THINKING LIKE A GOOD CONVERSATION. You have so much downtime when you are retired, and you spend much less time conversing with people than when you are in an office each day. Therefore, you tend to do less thinking. The mind is like any other muscle; you have to work it daily to keep it sharp. It would be very easy to lose a little of that sharpness without even realizing it. I'm reading, playing chess, doing *The New York Times* crossword puzzle—anything I can to keep my mind active. And I talk to anybody who will listen.

—BOB MAGYARICS
CALLA, OHIO
YEARS RETIRED: 2

A MAJOR CONCERN OF THE RETIREMENT YEARS is the fear
of Alzheimer's disease. Most of us try to exercise our brains.
I play Scrabble several times a week. I do a 500- or
1,000-piece jigsaw puzzle every month or so. Even
so, old, well-used words drop out of the mind
suddenly in the middle of a sentence like a
slippery fish.

—ANONYMOUS
SAVOY, ILLINOIS
YEARS RETIRED: 17

* * * * * * * *

AFTER I RETIRED, I became really interested in playing rac-
quetball. I had played off and on before, but I got serious
about it after I retired. I am a very competitive person by
nature, and I didn't like the fact that I wasn't as good as I
could have been because I didn't have the chance to work at
it. Now I play every day and enter about four or five tournaments a year.

—DAVID FELZKE
MORGANTOWN, WEST VIRGINIA
YEARS RETIRED: 5

* * * * * * * *

TAKE CARE OF YOURSELF. I see other people my age who are
not able to get out of the house. I am in good health and am
able to do what I want in retirement. I fish. I go hunting and
off-roading.

—J.L.
CLIMAX SPRINGS, MISSOURI
YEARS RETIRED: 10

AT MY AGE, the most important thing to eat is prunes. Prunes, prunes, and more prunes.

—FRED MATHEIS
DEERFIELD, OHIO
YEARS RETIRED: 10

* * * * * * * *

READ MAGAZINES AND BOOKS, and listen to books in your car. Keep the circuits going. Don't just sit around in an utterly passive way. Don't wait for the doctor to give you the pill that's going to keep you going until you're 98. You have to work on this yourself.

—EUGENE C. BIANCHI
ATHENS, GEORGIA
YEARS RETIRED: 5

* * * * * * * *

YOUTH HAS CONFIDENCE, CURIOSITY, and enthusiasm. If you can maintain those three things in life, you can be as youthful as you want to be.

—MICHAEL CREEDMAN
SAN FRANCISCO, CALIFORNIA

* * * * * * * *

I'VE GONE TO CURVES REGULARLY for the last three years. That has really helped me stay in shape, and I've realized that it gets me out of the house every day. Then, once I'm out, I do other errands and activities.

—ANONYMOUS
WOODBURY, MINNESOTA
YEARS RETIRED: 9

I THINK EVERYBODY SHOULD STRETCH. I do my stretches every morning and every night. I picture myself praying to Mecca, where my legs are tucked under me and I'm bent forward on the floor. My arms are stretched over my head and my spine is in perfect alignment. It keeps me limber.

—MENDELL PETER SPARKS
SPRINGFIELD, MISSOURI
YEARS RETIRED: 15

* * * * * * * *

AS YOUNG AS YOU FEEL

Studies show that spending time around young people helps keep the older generation energized and mentally stimulated. As a result, college towns are a growing retirement destination.

* * * * * * * *

WHEN YOU RETIRE, especially in a retirement community, there is a temptation to become an alcoholic. You can sit out with the neighbors every evening and drink. So we have to watch that. There is also a danger of getting fat. We eat out all the time, probably 16 out of 21 meals per week. Restaurant food typically isn't healthy, so you have to keep doing exercises and making good choices about eating.

—FRANK HAWK
LAKELAND, FLORIDA
YEARS RETIRED: 3

EXERCISE IS IMPORTANT TO STAYING HEALTHY. I exercise in a pool three times a week. I stretch and work my muscles. It helps my joints and circulation. I also mow my lawn every three days or so to get exercise.

—E.M.W.
SPRINGFIELD, MISSOURI
YEARS RETIRED: 12

* * * * * * * *

I'M REALLY INTO WALKING TO STAY IN SHAPE, but many people walk too slowly to get the full benefits. To improve your health, you need to walk fast enough to elevate your heart rate. You can measure your rate of exertion with something called the talk test: If you can speak easily in full sentences while walking, you're not working hard enough; if you can barely get a word out, you're pushing too hard. Look for something in the middle. It's helpful if you are walking with someone, because you want to be able to have at least a little bit of conversation back and forth.

—BOB PHILLIPS
HARRISONBURG, VIRGINIA
YEARS RETIRED: 4

* * * * * * * *

GO TO A CHIROPRACTOR! He can straighten you out. I believe so many ailments that affect older people can be avoided if they were properly aligned. The spine is everything. And the older you get, the more you slump.

—AARON
ST. PETERSBURG, FLORIDA
YEARS RETIRED: 2

TENNIS, EVERYONE!

YOU GET SO MUCH MORE OF A CARDIO workout playing tennis. No sport where they give you a cart to drive around is doing much for you physically.

—BARRY FITTERER
CUMBERLAND, MARYLAND
YEARS RETIRED: 3

* * * * * * * *

ONE OF MY NEIGHBORS TOOK UP TENNIS after retirement and, by the age of 81, has become a pretty great tennis player. We had a coed doubles tournament where the ages of the two partners had to equal at least 100. Mostly, it was teams composed of two people in their 50s, or maybe 60s and 40s. Well, the 81-year-old found a partner who was a 25-year-old tennis coach, and they wiped everybody else off the courts!

—LORI
CHARLESTON, SOUTH CAROLINA

* * * * * * * *

I PREFER TENNIS TO GOLF. I just can't get past the goofy attire that those old guys wear playing golf. And you've got all that walking up and down hills and in and out of the woods. At least if you play it the way I do.

—BILL DAUGHERTY
FROSTBURG, MARYLAND
YEARS RETIRED: 9

THE ONLY WAY TO STAY FIT AT ALL is to watch what you eat. The good thing is that I find I don't have the appetite I had when I was younger. I also seem to have lost my sweet tooth. Luckily, all my other teeth are still intact. You have to eat right so you can stick around to see your grandchildren grow up.

—A.P.
BOARDMAN, OHIO
YEARS RETIRED: 10

MAKE THE MOST OF IT

Here are some basic steps you can take to ensure a healthier and longer life:

- Eat lots of fresh fruits and vegetables, whole grains, lean meats, fish, and low-fat or no-fat dairy. Avoid sugars and saturated and trans fats.
- Talk with your physician about taking vitamins.
- Exercise for at least 30 minutes every day—walking, yard work, and playing with your grandkids count!
- Manage stress through exercise, stretching, relaxation, breathing, or medication, if necessary.
- Visit your doctor for regular checkups.
- Check your cholesterol and screen for cancers and other diseases that can be treated with early detection.

IF YOU GARDEN, you can eat healthier because you can eat the stuff you grow. I didn't have time for that before I stopped working, but now I have a certified green thumb. I grow tomatoes, potatoes, cucumbers, beans, corn; you name it, I grow it. And it saves me money on food.

—ROBIN LALLY
GREENFORD, OHIO
YEARS RETIRED: 1

* * * * * * * *

I'M EATING WHATEVER I WANT. What's the worst thing that could happen? I could die? That's going to happen soon enough anyway. I want to enjoy myself. Your later years are not the time to start watching what you eat. You should have been doing that when you were younger. Plus, every time you see them talking to some 100-year-old person on the news, and they ask them what is the secret to longevity, those people never say healthy eating. They always say they spent their lives living on booze and cigarettes. I'm on my way to 100.

—TIM SCHADE
UNITY, OHIO
YEARS RETIRED: 1

* * * * * * * *

KEEP FRIENDS WHO ARE A VARIETY OF AGES. I have friends who are in their 40s and friends who are 10 years older than I am. With some friends, I often see they get more and more morose as their old friends die off.

—MICHAEL CREEDMAN
SAN FRANCISCO, CALIFORNIA

I READ A STUDY OF 1,000 PEOPLE who continued to work at the age of 70 and beyond. It found that this group was more than twice as likely to be alive at the age of 82 than those who had retired and weren't working at the beginning of the study.

—ARTHUR KOFF
CHICAGO, ILLINOIS

* * * * * * *

MIND-BODY CONNECTION

More and more research shows that the key to keeping your mind sharp as you age is staying physically active.

* * * * * * *

THIS IS ONE WOMAN THAT YOU'RE NEVER GOING to find in some spinning class. I spent my whole life running around from one thing to the next. Working, taking kids here and there—you name it. Now is the time for me to put my feet up and relax.

—BEA BETTERS
POLAND, OHIO

* * * * * * *

STAY ACTIVE AS YOU GET OLDER; you just rust if you don't.

—DEE EYRE
JACKSONVILLE, TEXAS
YEARS RETIRED: 6

DO WHAT YOU CAN TO STAY IN SHAPE. If you don't feel good, you can't enjoy anything in life. Personally, I don't feel as much like being active if I haven't taken care of myself. If you join an exercise group for seniors, they never push you too hard because they are afraid of killing you. They treat you with kid gloves, and that's just fine by me.

—WALKER EDWARDS
CANFIELD, OHIO

* * * * * * * *

I GO TO CHURCH REGULARLY, but not necessarily at the times when everyone else goes. Sometimes I go when the place is empty, and I just sit quietly in a pew. I'm not praying, really, but just thinking about life. It's like meditation. When I walk out, I feel refreshed and stress-free. I believe it plays a big part in keeping me mentally and physically healthy.

—AARON
ST. PETERSBURG, FLORIDA
YEARS RETIRED: 2

* * * * * * * *

MY MENTAL HEALTH IS GOOD BECAUSE I don't sit at home; I go to my office every day. If I stayed home, I probably would think about the misery of old age instead of what I'm going to write next and what to do with the next chapter in the book I'm working on. It doesn't help my physical health, though. I don't think writing will help my prostate.

—RICHARD BING, M.D.
PASADENA, CALIFORNIA
YEARS RETIRED: 3

GOLF FOR LIFE

GOLF IS A GREAT COMBINATION of relaxation and exercise. And it gets me out of the house. I think my wife and I both like that part of it.

—ELMER GANTZ
POLAND, OHIO

• • • • • • • •

I LIKE GOLF BECAUSE I WANT A SPORT where I can go out with my friends and BS a little and drink a little. You can't do either of those things while you're running back and forth across a tennis court. Leave that sport to the weekend warriors who still have jobs to get back to on the weekdays.

—GEORGE ALLEN
FROSTBURG, MARYLAND
YEARS RETIRED: 1

• • • • • • • •

TRY TO MAINTAIN A SENSE OF HUMOR ABOUT GOLF. Don't take it too seriously. I never wrapped a golf club around a tree. But the better I got, the more relaxed I got, and now I can really enjoy it. That's good life advice, too: Don't be too hard on yourself; have a sense of humor about things.

—ROY CLARY
BROOKLYN, NEW YORK
YEARS RETIRED: 1

I PLAY GOLF AND TENNIS. There is no comparison as to which is the better sport for retirees. Tennis kills you. It's exhausting and it's easy to get injured. Golf, on the other hand, you can play for the rest of your life.

—GARY GALLAGHER
WILLIAMSON, WEST VIRGINIA
YEARS RETIRED: 1

• • • • • • • •

SOMEONE ONCE TOLD ME, "Put a golf club in your hand, and you'll play it the rest of your life." You know what? They were right!

—M.K.
SOUTHPORT, CONNECTICUT
YEARS RETIRED: 12

DON'T CUT CORNERS ON EATING. Too many of my retired friends have fallen into the frozen dinner trap, or else they're loading up on lots of processed bakery goods. It's a fact: What you eat totally affects your health. My solution? I grow a big garden, and I eat a lot of vegetables. I've never felt better in my life, and the garden is fun to tend to.

—ANONYMOUS
LOS ANGELES, CALIFORNIA
YEARS RETIRED: 10

* * * * * * * *

THERE'S A LOT OF WONDERFUL SPIRITUAL WISDOM out there in religious and ancient traditions. I try to pull from them all. I read the Tao Te Ching, the Bhagavata, and other texts. The point is to find wisdom that can both enrich one's inner life and make one more compassionate in serving the outside world.

—EUGENE C. BIANCHI
ATHENS, GEORGIA
YEARS RETIRED: 5

* * * * * * * *

I HAVE 40 ACRES. IT'S QUIET. A school bus and a car went by this morning. I was in New York City a couple of weeks ago, and I thought, this is cruel and unusual punishment. Living quietly is, for me, a good thing. Other people love the tumult of the city; I'm not one of them. My wife and I intend to live here until we die, if we can.

—ROBERT L. ZIMDAHL
FORT COLLINS, COLORADO
YEARS RETIRED: 1

CONTINUE TO FIND SPECIAL TIMES THAT YOU and your wife can share. I'm talking about sex: A good sex life as you grow older is just as important to me now as when I was a young man. It's certainly different now. But I think as I grow older I'm valuing love more. Sex is a part of love.

—ROY CLARY
BROOKLYN, NEW YORK
YEARS RETIRED: 1

* * * * * * * *

I'VE ENJOYED GOOD HEALTH BECAUSE I'm a natural optimist. It's also important to know that one who is not a natural optimist can learn to be one. Learning to be one is important and helps people to survive and live healthier and happier and longer.

—FRANCES LOMAS FELDMAN
PASADENA, CALIFORNIA
YEARS RETIRED: 24

* * * * * * * *

WORK IN YOUR YARD, read all those books you've been stacking up, volunteer in your community, go traveling. Don't just sit at home.

—SUSAN
TAYLOR, TEXAS
YEARS RETIRED: 3

IF YOU DON'T FIND SOMETHING to keep your mind active, it will wither and die, just like any other unused muscle in the body. I play chess every single day. And I win.

—RALPH DINARDO
STRUTHERS, OHIO
YEARS RETIRED: 4

* * * * * * * *

I AM TAKING YOGA CLASSES AND WORKING with a fitness trainer. I guess you could say that mind and body have become more of a focus for me, and I find that very positive.

—ELAINE
TORONTO, ONTARIO

Generations: On Family & Responsibilities

Now that you're retired, you come first: Do what you want to do, go wherever you like, spend your money however you decide. There's just one little thing—your family. They still need you, want you, and can think of lots of ways you could be really helpful. Of course, you need to set limits. But it's a funny thing: Family life may never have been better. So enjoy yourself with your family, and cherish those chores—it all adds up to more good times.

BE SELF-RELIANT. Try not to rely so much on the family. Retired people who rely on their family usually are disappointed. The young family members, no matter how much they love the old man, they have a thing about not being bothered too much. Be independent as much as possible. I rely on my family, but I have to keep aware that this is not a desirable thing.

—RICHARD BING, M.D.
PASADENA, CALIFORNIA
YEARS RETIRED: 3

* * * * * * * *

BEING ABLE TO SPEND SOME TIME WITH YOUR KIDS and their kids is the best part of being retired.

—PATRICK CALIENDO
POLAND, OHIO

* * * * * * * *

WE BOUGHT SOME LAKESHORE PROPERTY NEARBY, which has allowed us to spend a lot of time with our kids and grandkids. When we were looking at property, we considered something in Arizona or Florida, but that would have meant spending less time with the grandkids, and we didn't want that. The grandkids see we all have fun, but there's also work to do. There are a lot of oak trees on the property, for example, so that's become a family activity: When it's too cold to go in the lake, the whole family rakes leaves.

—ANONYMOUS
WOODBURY, MINNESOTA
YEARS RETIRED: 9

NOW THAT I AM RETIRED, I take care of my two grandsons three days a week. I couldn't bear to think of them going to day care. I enjoy having them around. I was working when my kids were growing up. It's nice to be able to relax and play with them.

—DONNA HANAFIN
NIXA, MISSOURI
YEARS RETIRED: 4

* * * * * * * *

FAMILY AFFAIR

Some retirees are persuading their families to move into new multigenerational communities. Designed to recreate small towns where families lived in close proximity, they include schools, water slides, golf courses, and more.

* * * * * * * *

YOU HAVE TO REMEMBER YOUR ROLE AS GRANDPARENT, and it is *not* to be involved in the kids' lives every day. My son and his wife live in Michigan, and I try to see them as often as I can without becoming a nuisance. They come in for Easter and Christmas, and I usually go out there for a week in the summer. I think it's nice to be somewhat close but not too close. They need their space, too, so that they can raise their family.

—ELLEN WAYNE
BOARDMAN, OHIO

WE HAVE NEIGHBORS WHO WERE RECENTLY MARRIED in their 60s, each with grown children and grandchildren. They went on their honeymoon right after the wedding. Literally the day they returned—and without any warning—the new bride's godchild (a great-niece of hers) was dropped on their doorstep, and they were named the sole custodians. So as retirees, they were plopped right back into the life of elementary schools, homework, sleepovers, kids! At times it's overwhelming, but we also see how much they are in love and how they make the best out of having a surprise family so late in life.

—MARTY
CHICAGO, ILLINOIS

* * * * * * * *

I HAVE SIX CHILDREN AND 11 GRANDCHILDREN, with more probably on the way. I love being around the grandchildren, and my kids often ask me to babysit them while they go out. But I have found that there are times when I have to say no to babysitting. At first I didn't want to upset my kids by turning them down. But I found that they are more understanding than I gave them credit for. They know Mom is not a spring chicken anymore. And I simply don't have the energy to chase the grandchildren around as much as I'd like. I think it's important to chip in and help out when you can, but you have to know your limitations.

—EILEEN MCCARTHY
PITTSBURGH, PENNSYLVANIA
YEARS RETIRED: 8

SIX MONTHS BEFORE I RETIRED, we had been planning on selling our house and moving to Florida. At the time, my wife was complaining that we were never going to have grandchildren. I told her, "You know, when I retire, one daughter will tell us she's expecting, and another will tell us the following year." Sure enough, at my retirement party, our daughter stood up and said, "Dad doesn't know it yet, but he's going to be a grandfather." Eighteen months after that, she had another child, and our oldest daughter had one, too. We didn't wind up moving.

—GALEN R. REIL
RICHMOND, VIRGINIA
YEARS RETIRED: 5

* * * * * * * *

I LOVE TO SEE MY GRANDKIDS, and we have them over a lot. But sometimes I say, "Sure, we'll have them over, but not the whole day because I have a lot of errands to do." If I can't do it, I just say so. What are they going to do?

—JANET
MINNEAPOLIS, MINNESOTA
YEARS RETIRED: 10

* * * * * * * *

HAVE YOUR OWN LIFE. Do not expect to live your kids' lives when you retire. Do not depend on others to entertain you. If you have your own life and interests, you will be a more interesting person, and people will want to be around you.

—K.J.H.
WESTERVILLE, OHIO

IT'S GOOD TO HAVE FAMILY AROUND, but not necessary. Be on your own. You just can't depend on other people, whether relatives or friends, to handle your life for you. I still live life like I did in my 20s or 30s.

—BOB RICH
CHARLOTTE, NORTH CAROLINA
YEARS RETIRED: 4

* * * * * * * *

USE THE COMPUTER TO STAY IN TOUCH. One of my boys is local, but the other is not. I have found that with computer innovations like the Internet, e-mail, and digital photos, I can stay in touch with them much more easily than my parents could with me when I left home. My son sends me photos of his kids in an e-mail about once a week so I can really see how they are growing. It does make me feel closer to them.

—RAY BALLAST
BOARDMAN, OHIO

* * * * * * * *

OUR YOUNGEST GRANDCHILD, who is now 18 months old, spends every Tuesday at our house. It's fun to be with him when he's learning so many new things. It really does help you bond. When my daughter first went back to work, six weeks after he was born, I just couldn't stand to see him with a babysitter all the time, so we had him every day for two and a half months. But that just totally wore us out. One day a week now is perfect.

—CYNTHIA
ST. PAUL, MINNESOTA
YEARS RETIRED: 8

SOUND FAMILIAR?

Some common issues for folks in my age range are these:

1. Many of us are caretakers for parents whose financial situation is precarious; their vulnerability is ours. Uncertainty regarding their longevity and a need for resources is a major factor.

2. While some of my siblings are quite stable, with no likelihood of needing anything from me, a couple of others could get tricky. We have arranged for health insurance for one because, despite her age and risk factors, insurance was not a priority for her. Getting the insurance for her was for our benefit because we felt if she got sick, we would have to do something.

3. Getting children to an independent, secure situation is a gift. But it's not always easy to do.

I feel reasonably secure in terms of having the basics covered, all the financial management stuff. But it is the life crises from so many possible different directions that disturb me.

—Anonymous
Omaha, Nebraska

IT IS A GOOD SYMBIOTIC RELATIONSHIP, now that I'm home for my teenage daughter. I gain by having the emotional connection, and she gains by having the constant support. For instance, she's in a school play, with rehearsals every day. The kids were expected to go home after school at 2 p.m. and come back at 5 p.m. And she also has started taking voice lessons in the afternoon to get ready for the play. How could she do all this without me around? Now that I can drive her, I get a feeling of really being there for her—and it's an excuse to spend some quality time together.

—FRED
MILLER PLACE, NEW YORK
YEARS RETIRED: 2

* * * * * * * *

I WAS MARRIED FOR OVER 50 YEARS when my wife died. My advice for someone who loses his spouse: Don't make an effort to find someone else. Some old people do a terrible thing: They lose their spouse and try to start all over again. Self-reliance is one of the most important things. My secret is simply that I love to do things that have to do with art and communications. I spend my time doing these things.

—RICHARD BING, M.D.
PASADENA, CALIFORNIA
YEARS RETIRED: 3

FAMILY TIME

Surveys confirm that many retirees find the most enjoyable activity to be spending more time with their adult children and grandchildren.

Dos & Don'ts: Words to Remember

One thing about the hundreds of retirees who contributed to these chapters: they like to pass along what they've learned, even if they just learned it yesterday. Along with good advice, there are plenty of warnings and admonitions. For them, the retirement years may be full of surprising experiences. Read on for inspirational (and humorous) views.

IF YOU START DRESSING OLD, YOU *ARE* OLD. No matter how old she got, my mother never started dressing like my grandmother. She never dressed like an old person. I'll never stop wearing jeans and sneakers no matter how old I get.

> —L.H.
> BAZETTA, OHIO
> YEARS RETIRED: 1

* * * * * * * *

ENJOY YOUR SPOUSE. My wife, Molly, and I have a lot of fun; we fish and do things together. Discover new activities that you both enjoy—it will keep you young at heart!

> —JAMES KOLB
> JACKSONVILLE, TEXAS
> YEARS RETIRED: 15

* * * * * * * *

INDULGE YOURSELF. Enjoy listening to old-time jazz, read two papers a day, watch CNBC and C-SPAN, and even spend a whole afternoon with a juicy mystery. Do all the things you never could do before.

> —T.S.
> TAMPA, FLORIDA
> YEARS RETIRED: 12

* * * * * * * *

YOU SHOULD GET UP AND HUNT for something good, not something bad.

> —MOLLY KOLB
> JACKSONVILLE, TEXAS
> YEARS RETIRED: 10

MAKE PLANS WITH OLD FRIENDS. Recently, the girls from my high school graduating class got together for a reunion. You have to do things like that just to keep excited about life.

—JANET
PARMA, OHIO
YEARS RETIRED: 3

* * * * * * * *

AVOID THE VOID

Take steps to make friends outside of your workplace so you don't find yourself missing the daily social interaction.

* * * * * * * *

WHILE YOU ARE ALIVE, WORRY ABOUT LIFE: You'll have plenty of time to worry about death when you are dead. I'm a big believer in the idea of self-fulfilling prophecies. I've been around too many people my age who spend too much time worrying about death. I believe that if you think about death, you will bring it on quicker. There's no need to worry about it because it's going to happen no matter what. No one has figured out a way to cheat death yet. I was at a meeting where this older gentleman told the group at least 10 times that he knew his days were numbered. That was all he could think about.

—OTIS REQUISH
POLAND, OHIO
YEARS RETIRED: 2

How to Love Your Retirement

DO FOR OTHERS, AND YOU WILL FORGET your own ailments. That is a big thing with retired people; when you're sick and you think negative thoughts, it just drags you down. You've got to get up every day with a positive attitude.

—JAMES KOLB
JACKSONVILLE, TEXAS
YEARS RETIRED: 15

* * * * * * * *

TAKE CONTROL

People who retire by choice enjoy happier retirements than those who are forced to stop working, whether due to illness or layoffs. The difference in satisfaction levels can be seen for up to 10 years.

* * * * * * * *

DON'T TRAVEL BY YOURSELF IN A CAR LONG-DISTANCE because you are likely to kill yourself. The craziest thing I ever did since retiring was to drive from Norman, Oklahoma, to Palm Beach, Florida, in one stretch by myself. I only stopped to get gasoline because I wanted to get home. I couldn't stay awake for the last hundred or so miles, and I was numb when I got there. It was a stupid thing to do.

—STAN
NORMAN, OKLAHOMA
YEARS RETIRED: 20

I REALIZED WITHIN THE FIRST WEEK OF RETIREMENT that taking care of myself in the morning—brushing my teeth, washing up, getting dressed—was important, not just something to rush through because I had to get to work. It was important to honor myself enough to do those things. And when I did, it made things more normal and pleasant. Getting dressed, I am more apt to experience the day spontaneously. I am ready for everything, to go out if I need to, whether to go to the store or to run errands, or just to take a walk. Sitting around in sweatpants or pajamas is not conducive to that.

—MICHAEL
SAYVILLE, NEW YORK
YEARS RETIRED: 1

* * * * * * * *

STAY CONNECTED. I enjoy using the Internet. I follow the stock market quite a bit. I read a lot of newspapers online. It saves me money because I don't have to buy a lot of newspapers, and it keeps me informed of world events.

—ANONYMOUS
SAN FRANCISCO, CALIFORNIA

* * * * * * * *

IF OTHERS SUGGEST YOU'RE TOO OLD TO DO SOMETHING, thumb your nose at them and do it. Find what makes you happy and do it.

—EMILY KIMBALL
RICHMOND, VIRGINIA

THE BEST THING ABOUT RETIREMENT

I CAN DO WHAT I WANT. I play golf, smoke cigars, and travel with my wife. Also, now I get to read books. When I was working, I never had time for that.

—DAN PISANI
MERIDEN, CONNECTICUT
YEARS RETIRED: 1

• • • • • • • •

I'VE BECOME MUCH MORE INVOLVED WITH MY FAMILY. I spend more time with my grandkids, and at the end of the day, this is what's important.

—DOROTHY DURBIN GAUDIN
TORONTO, ONTARIO
YEARS RETIRED: 10

• • • • • • • •

I'M ABLE TO PURSUE MY TWO LOVES: music and gardening. I play the piano every day now and have season tickets to the symphony. I go to Duke Chapel every week, too, to hear the music there, which is amazing. I'm also able to spend more time in my yard gardening.

—M.A.R.
DURHAM, NORTH CAROLINA
YEARS RETIRED: 8

I DO THINGS WHEN I want to do them, not when I have to do them.

>—M.K.
>SOUTHPORT, CONNECTICUT
>YEARS RETIRED: 12

* * * * * * * *

THE BEST PART IS SLEEPING IN AND SHOWERING, dressing, eating breakfast at my leisure. The worst part is that everyone thinks, "Oh, she is retired, I will just ask her to do this. She has so much time on her hands."

>—C.R.
>SAN ANTONIO, TEXAS
>YEARS RETIRED: 1

* * * * * * * *

RECONNECTING WITH FRIENDS AND CLASSMATES from years ago is very rewarding.

>—ARTHUR KOFF
>CHICAGO, ILLINOIS

YOU'VE WAITED ALL YOUR LIFE FOR THIS MOMENT. Do you have something you can hardly wait to start doing? You'd better! I have a friend who ran an envelope company and traveled all the time. Upon retiring about 10 years ago, he stated, "I never want to have to travel anywhere again." He hasn't. As a consequence, his wife, who never got to travel, has been left sitting at home, watching him deteriorate physically and mentally. He would do nothing but sit in the backyard. A few months ago, he came to me and said, "You know, I've sure been selfish these last 10 years. I've wasted both my and my wife's few years left. When I traveled, it was always to the same few places and towns. Now I realize there's a whole world out there we could have been seeing." They spent a month making arrangements to go overseas and see Europe. He died just before they were to leave.

—J.L.
DALLAS, TEXAS
YEARS RETIRED: 15

SET GOALS FOR YOURSELF. Whether you set them monthly or yearly, it's important to keep yourself focused on something attainable, tangible. It's easy to get lulled into a life of inactivity with very little personal production. Each year I set goals for personal wealth, time spent on charity causes, and health factors like weight and cholesterol levels.

——MARK HEDNASLER
YOUNGSTOWN, OHIO
YEARS RETIRED: 4

FOUR-LEGGED FRIENDS

Looking for a distraction now that you have all this time to yourself? Consider getting a pet. Research shows that pet owners are 22% happier than the rest of the population.

IT'S IMPORTANT TO HAVE FRIENDS OF ALL AGES. The other day, I wrote three sympathy cards and I thought, "I have to get younger friends!" It's really important to connect with younger people; I do it through church activities and the gym, and I try to keep in contact with people I used to work with who are a little bit younger than I am.

——HARRIET SMITH
SAN ANTONIO, TEXAS
YEARS RETIRED: 2

THE MOST IMPORTANT THING IS TO STAY AWAY from the "I can't do that because I'm too old" mindset. Thinking like that can be hazardous to your health. I read twice a week to elementary school kids. Being around all of that energy and enthusiasm makes me feel young.

—ANONYMOUS
BALTIMORE, MARYLAND
YEARS RETIRED: 13

* * * * * * * *

DON'T BUY INTO THE AGEISM IN OUR CULTURE. Many people still see us as old and incapable of many things that we are more than capable of. If someone tells me I play tennis like a 55-year-old when I am 73, I don't consider that a compliment. I look them straight in the eye and say that an older person who has played tennis all her life can play tennis like this at 73. It is an ageist statement that assumes that one shouldn't be able to play tennis that well at 73. Baloney. People said I was too old to bike across America. I had osteoporosis. How would I get over the mountains? Well, I tell them that we might not be fast, but we have stamina and can outlast the best of them. Ageism is like racism, and it limits us.

—EMILY KIMBALL
RICHMOND, VIRGINIA

Wisdom for the Ages: Lessons Learned & More

This "Third Age" is a natural time to grow philosophical. Although they look both backwards and forwards, many respondents still say they strive to live in the present moment; that's good advice for any age. Read on for more wisdom.

WHEN I RETIRED, SOME OF MY COLLEAGUES asked me what I was going to do first. I told them I didn't know, but I knew what I *wasn't* going to do: get a divorce, take up drinking, start smoking, or become a gambler, because they are all expensive, both to your health and to your pocketbook! I worked hard to have great golden years, and I'm not going to blow it now.

—JIM EYRE
JACKSONVILLE, TEXAS
YEARS RETIRED: 6

* * * * * * * *

ATTITUDE IS THE KEY TO SUCCESSFUL RETIREMENT. You don't have to do things that cost a lot of money. I love going on picnics, taking walks, enjoying nature. That doesn't cost anything. People get so caught up in the traveling, in thinking you have to go halfway around the world, when you can just enjoy the place where you are.

—ANONYMOUS
ST. PAUL, MINNESOTA

* * * * * * * *

HERE'S ONE THING I'VE LEARNED ABOUT RETIREMENT: You're not going to get your photographs organized into albums. People think that they're going to do that when they're retired, but if they're not interested enough to have done it before, they're not going to do it when they're retired, either.

—JANET
MINNEAPOLIS, MINNESOTA
YEARS RETIRED: 10

I REALLY MISS SEEING ALL THE PEOPLE I used to work with every day. I recently went back to my work for a retirement party. I realized that while I missed my friends, I didn't miss the BS. It makes me appreciate being out of there.

—LAWRENCE "BIMP" LAYMAN
HARRISONBURG, VIRGINIA
YEARS RETIRED: 1

* * * * * * * *

DON'T THINK OF IT AS RETIRING FROM LIFE; it is just another phase of life. Take the energy you put into your work and put it into an activity you truly enjoy: taking courses, doing pottery, writing poetry, whatever. It is most important to give it your all and just consider it another aspect of your life.

—BEVERLY ZEIDENBERG
BETHESDA, MARYLAND
YEARS RETIRED: 2

* * * * * * * *

RETIREMENT IS HEARING THE BIRDS SING, not having to lock my dogs up and leave them alone all day, sleeping in, long casual showers, yummy home cooking, not having to buy groceries with all the working crowd, no work evaluations, watering my plants as I drink my morning cup of coffee, time to pray and reflect, seeing my family more. Retirement is about making my own decisions at my own pace and having time to enjoy the world around me.

—C.R.
SAN ANTONIO, TEXAS
YEARS RETIRED: 1

RETIREMENT IS FREEDOM. I do what I want to do. It's not that I hated working, but it was an obligation. I'm able to enjoy life more because I have the freedom to do what I want, and I'm young and healthy enough to enjoy it.

—JAMES EVANS
REPUBLIC, MISSOURI
YEARS RETIRED: 5

* * * * * * * *

WHAT DO I MISS SINCE I RETIRED? A paycheck, my boss, and the co-workers/friends whom I saw every day. But what a joy to just sit here in the morning, drink that cup of coffee, and see the younger people on their way to work.

—RUTH BEARDEN
JACKSONVILLE, TEXAS
YEARS RETIRED: 16

* * * * * * * *

I WORK IN RADIATION THERAPY, and I can't tell you the number of people who have retired and then spent the next week with me getting radiation therapy treatments. I'm sure I wasn't the person they planned on retiring with. Don't put off all the fun trips, showing people love, living life while you are living day to day. Retirement can be very fun, and it's important to remember the saying, "Life is the journey." So many people don't get that concept until the end of their lives, and by then you cannot go back and change anything you wished you would have done. Make every day count!

—K.J.H.
WESTERVILLE, OHIO

EVER HEAR THE ONE ABOUT THE OLD COUPLE who were in bed together? The old wife raised the covers to look at her man and said, "You didn't save anything for retirement, did you?"

—KENNETH R. WADE
GATLINBURG, TENNESSEE
YEARS RETIRED: 1

* * * * * * *

IN THE LONG RUN, doing a good job of raising your children is one of the best contributions you can make to the future of humankind. You never get to stop being a parent. You think one day they'll go off to college, get a job, and get on with their own lives. But they're never off your mind. You accumulate all this great advice that they don't want. But it's good to keep in touch, and it's good to love them and let them know that. For most of us, that's probably our major contribution to the world. Love your wife, take care of your children, take care of your community.

—ROBERT L. ZIMDAHL
FORT COLLINS, COLORADO
YEARS RETIRED: 1

* * * * * * * *

THE THING ABOUT RETIREMENT that has surprised me most is that after many, many years of being independent and having a lot of time to myself, I enjoy having my spouse around!

—NOLA SMITH
TAMPA, FLORIDA
YEARS RETIRED: 25

RETIREMENT IS LIKE A VACATION FOR THE REST OF YOUR LIFE.
I'm happy that we had five good years together before my
husband got sick and passed away in 2002. Getting older
makes you more fully appreciate what you have, and you
have the time to enjoy it!

> —BARBARA DICKERSON
> OLD MINES, MISSOURI
> YEARS RETIRED: 15

* * * * * * * *

IF YOU LET THE DAY UNFOLD, it has its own music. You just
have to sit and listen to it. There's so much beauty in not
planning the day. I think that's where I am now, and why I
can say I'm happy.

> —MICHAEL
> SAYVILLE, NEW YORK
> YEARS RETIRED: 1

* * * * * * * *

WHEN YOU LOSE A FRIEND, make another one.

> —MICHAEL CREEDMAN
> SAN FRANCISCO, CALIFORNIA

* * * * * * * *

KEEP REACHING OUT TO PEOPLE and respond to them when
they reach out to you. Be active. Don't sit in a corner and
read or watch TV. That's not the way to really enjoy life.

> —FRANCES LOMAS FELDMAN
> PASADENA, CALIFORNIA
> YEARS RETIRED: 24

IF THE GOOD LORD MADE ANYTHING BETTER than sex and retirement, then he kept it for Himself! It just gets better and better!

—CHALMERS GABLE
MARION, TEXAS
YEARS RETIRED: 5

. . . .

LIFE IS VERY PRECIOUS. People don't take enough time to look at the sky and the stars and the moon and hug a tree once in a while. The other day I saw a kid kissing a tree. I thought, That's fantastic. What wonderful things the trees do for us; they clean the air and give us shade. We need to love each other and love our environment and our planet.

—ROY CLARY
BROOKLYN, NEW YORK
YEARS RETIRED: 1

. . . .

THE BIGGEST FEAR AS I MOVE FORWARD into retirement is becoming incapacitated, physically and/or mentally. I have no control over this (unless I do something stupid, like ski into the woods), so I have decided not to worry. I have planned as best I can long-term care insurance, wills, power of attorney, and so on. Beyond that, there is nothing that can be done. Now, I have put that fear aside and decided to enjoy whatever time is left to me doing what I love to do.

—PHIL MACKALL
ARLINGTON, VIRGINIA
YEARS RETIRED: 1

STRIVE FOR A POSITIVE ATTITUDE. Sinking into feeling sorry for oneself is a no-no.

—JoAnn
Joppa, Maryland
Years retired: 9

* * * * * * *

EVERY DAY, I WANT TO BE READY to experience whatever life throws my way.

—Michael
Sayville, New York
Years retired: 1

* * * * * * *

IN RETIREMENT, EVERY DAY IS SUNDAY. Who could complain about that?

—Anonymous
New York, New York

* * * * * * *

DON'T POSTPONE. We don't live in a solid state. Life is changing. Live in the now.

—Eugene C. Bianchi
Athens, Georgia
Years retired: 5

* * * * * * *

RETIREMENT IS LIKE A FLOWER: It is constantly opening.

—J.L.
Centralia, Washington
Years retired: 9

WHAT MOTIVATES ME NOW? Just getting out of bed and remaining healthy and getting to spend quality time with my seven grandchildren. And now having the time and the opportunity to be a good role model in their lives. Getting to play a large role in their lives is great. I have found that now I can commit so much time to them without having to worry about getting to bed at a certain time because I have to work the next day. I can give myself completely to them, and that's a very unburdening feeling. I want to be able to watch them all grow up and get married and have children of their own. I'm motivated by the chance to be a great-grandmother.

—J.E.
MORGANTOWN, WEST VIRGINIA
YEARS RETIRED: 2

* * * * * * * *

WHAT GETS ME OUT OF BED IN THE MORNING? The simple fact that I can.

—DAVID FELZKE
MORGANTOWN, WEST VIRGINIA
YEARS RETIRED: 5

* * * * * * * *

YOU NEVER SEE BEAUTY until you've got the time to look.

—BARBARA DICKERSON
OLD MINES, MISSOURI
YEARS RETIRED: 15

WHILE WE WERE VACATIONING IN CABO SAN LUCAS, MEXICO, last month, we came across this quotation, which I think is something to consider when retiring: "Life should not be a journey to the grave with the intention of arriving safely in an attractive and well-preserved body, but rather you should skid in sideways, chocolate in one hand, martini in the other, body thoroughly used up, totally worn out, and screaming, 'Woo hoo! What a ride!' Life is not measured by the number of breaths we take, but by the moments that take our breath away."

—KENNETH R. WADE
GATLINBURG, TENNESSEE
YEARS RETIRED: 1

INFORMATION AND LIFE
COACHING EXERCISES

PLAN FOR YOUR RETIREMENT IN FIVE EASY STEPS

Still wondering if now is the time to finally call it quits (or rather, call it a new beginning)? We all need a little push. Here are some helpful tips to send you on your way.

1. Take the time to thoughtfully design this next stage of your life—identify passions and activities you may not have had time to pursue until now. Think about what factors will give your life a sense of meaning and purpose.

2. Meet with an accountant or financial adviser to determine whether you can successfully meet the financial requirements associated with this plan.

3. Determine whether you want a "bridge" career—something to ease you out of the workforce—or to stop completely.

4. Create a wellness plan that includes an exercise and diet regimen to meet your individual needs as you "mature."

5. Develop and strengthen your emotional support networks—these relationships are critical to successful aging.

CHECKING UNDER THE HOOD: ARE YOU TAKING CARE OF YOURSELF?

So many of us put off taking care of ourselves while we are working full-time. No more excuses: Be honest with yourself in answering these questions and think about what you might do to better support yourself.

1. What is the current state of your general health?

2. Do you get enough sleep?

3. Do you wake up feeling refreshed?

4. Do your eating habits reflect your dietary requirements?

5. Do your eating habits keep you at or around your goal weight?

6. Have you had a health checkup in the past year?

7. Do you have a regular exercise routine that increases your heart rate for approximately 30 minutes? If so, how many times per week do you exercise?

8. How is your stress level? And what are some healthy ways you've found to deal with stress in your life?

LIFE BALANCE EXERCISE

The sections of the wheel on the next page represent a sense of balance and fulfillment. This exercise helps you understand how you are spending your time and how good you feel about various aspects of your life. It helps to identify what's working, what's not, and where you might want to begin to make some changes.

Regarding the center of the wheel as 0 and the outer edges as 10, rank your degree of satisfaction with each area by drawing a line to create a new outer edge. Use a different color for each piece of the pie. If these titles don't reflect your life, fill in your own. The new perimeter of the circle will illustrate the balance you have in your life. How bumpy would the ride be if this were a real wheel?

WHEEL OF BALANCE

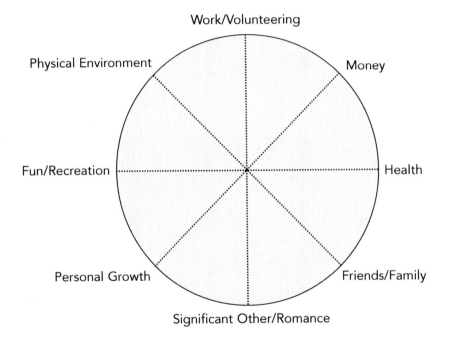

KNOW WHEN TO HOLD 'EM AND WHEN TO FOLD 'EM

aking lists is a powerful way to clarify your thoughts. Create this chart to help you visualize how you may make changes in the future. Indicate how you can begin to restructure and improve your life by listing activities that fit in each of the four categories below and on the next page.

HOLD ON	LET GO

PLANNING WORKSHEET

As you begin to plan for retirement, a funny thing happens: You tend to want to simplify. As you envision your future and develop new goals, explore how you might simplify your life on a global as well as an everyday basis.

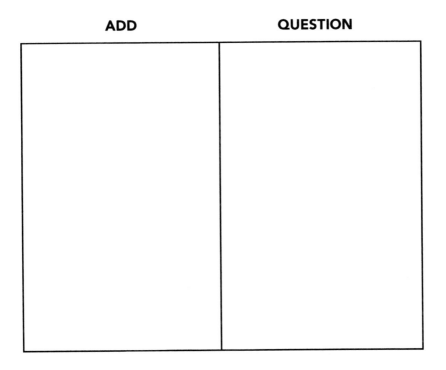

ADD   **QUESTION**

TO MOVE OR NOT TO MOVE: THAT IS THE QUESTION

After completing the Wheel of Balance exercise, take a look at how you rated your physical environment. Then investigate further by asking yourself these questions:

1. What do you like about your immediate neighborhood? Your town?

2. How do you feel about the current level of upkeep necessary for your home?

3. In thinking about your finances, does the overhead associated with maintaining your home significantly minimize other choices you make about things you would like to do?

4. What do you like about your current home? What would you change?

5. Think about other things you have wanted to do in your home—clean out the clutter, for instance?

6. Allow yourself to dream: Is there someplace or some type of living environment you've always wanted to experience but had too many responsibilities, forcing you to say no?

A COACH'S GUIDE TO MAKING YOUR WISDOM WORK FOR YOU

There's more to preparing for this next stage of life than financial planning and physical fitness. While you're getting organized, don't forget to accomplish some spring cleaning on your inner self. Here are some tools for the job:

1. Listen to messages you've gotten from your most significant mentors. These might include your third-grade teacher, a friend, a religious leader, and the like. Who are they and what core message resonated with you? How can you integrate that learning into your life?

2. The arts are a powerful tool for reflection and can open avenues for personal exploration and growth. Core meaning is expressed by all cultures through the use of music, poetry, art, and stories. Reconnect with some aspect of the arts and see what it teaches you. Have you always dreamed of singing? Painting? Writing?

3. Accept yourself inside and out. It takes courage to make peace with yourself, and the third stage of life is a gift of time and opportunity to develop increased clarity about what you choose to do and create with what you've got.

4. Identify your core passions and sense of purpose. Think about what gifts and talents you possess—even those you've never used before. Use these as a launching pad for designing the post-career life you'd like to lead.

ANNUAL GOAL-SETTING WORKSHEET

Think about where you would like to be in your life in one year. What goals do you want to achieve? Be realistic and don't bite off more than you can chew. Make your goals SMART: Specific, Measurable, Achievable, Realistic, and Time-oriented.

Date: _____

Work: _____

_____

_____

Family/Relationships: _____

_____

_____

Health/Fitness: _____

_____

_____

Spirituality:_____

_____

_____

_____

Civic Engagement: _____

_____

_____

Fun/Travel/Recreation:_____

_____

_____

Lifelong Learning: _____

Other: _____

_____

_____

_____

_____

_____

_____

_____

_____

_____

KEYS TO MAKING RETIREMENT THE BEST YEARS OF YOUR LIFE

1. *Understand yourself and what drives you.* Is your identity governed by your title at work? The stories we hear about people dropping dead the day after retirement are most often just urban legends, but some people do feel tremendous stress when they are cut off from an extremely important part of their lives. Let's face it; many of us spend more hours at work than anywhere else. Pre-plan a shift towards identifying yourself in a different way. Working with a life-transition coach is particularly helpful at this juncture; a coach can help crystallize just who you want to be, now that you are a grown-up!

2. *Before you leave your job, find activities that will be fulfilling.* One of the most satisfying and useful ways to support a change in identity from work to retirement is to try new things. Become a renaissance man or woman as you dabble in the arts, in travel, in all sorts of new activities. Or redirect your professional energies into a bridge career or volunteer job. Rather than identifying just one focus, allow yourself to explore and discover what you might like to do with your time; and, just as important, what you will shy away from.

3. *Understand and prepare for the natural change in family dynamics.* The anecdotes about retirement as today's number one threat to health may not be true, but the old

adage, "I married you for breakfast, but not for lunch," sure is. An unanticipated source of stress for retirees and their loved ones can be the tendency to want to spend all of their time together. Communication is vital—talk about expectations you each have about time spent together and shifting household responsibilities. Also consider the needs of extended family members: parents and children. They may be looking forward to spending more time with you or getting more help from you. How will this fit into your overall plan?

4. *Develop new social outlets.* Many of us develop friend-ships around the water cooler and miss that interaction once we retire. Having more time enables you to deepen existing relationships, attend to broken ones, and develop new friendships based on common interests and activities. Women tend to be more adept at this than men, but expanding social outlets is just as important for men once relationships are no longer centered around the office.

5. *Create a solid financial plan.* It's been estimated that retirees should expect to generate 80–100 percent of their pre-retirement income in order to maintain a comfortable lifestyle. This requires the 3 Ps: Planning, Perseverance, and Plenty of sources of income. Along with Social Security, Pension, IRA and 401K monies, look to make investments that will make a steady return.

NUMBERS DON'T LIE

*S*urprising but true: Most people nearing retirement age don't really know their net worth. This number is a crucial first step in determining if you are financially ready to retire. And if it turns out you still have some work to do, like most people, then there's no further excuse for delay. Here's a simple way to get started: Subtract your total debts from total assets to determine your net worth.

ASSETS	NAME/VALUE
Real Estate Holdings	
Automobiles	
Jewelry, Antiques, Art	
Money Market Funds	
Other Funds (CDs)	
Life Insurance	
IRA Accounts	
Pension/Profit Sharing Plans	
401K Plan	
Investments:	
Stocks	
Bonds	
Property	
Business Equity	
Trusts	
Other	
TOTAL ASSETS	

DEBTS	NAME/VALUE
Mortgage	
Loans	
car	
education	
home equity	
other	
Alimony/Child Support	
Credit Card Debt	
Other	
TOTAL DEBTS	
NET WORTH	

FINANCIAL CHECKUP FOR PRE-RETIREES

According to a Fidelity Management and Research report in 2004, a retiree's financial plan should yield an income stream of between 80–100 percent of pre-retirement income in order to live comfortably. The following questions will help you determine how close you are to that goal:

1. Determine your post-retirement lifestyle and associated expenses. Will you be traveling more or less? Eating out more or less? You will probably be spending more money on recreation. How do these changes compare to your current cost of living?

2. Determine your specific retirement benefits. These include Social Security, pensions, IRA's, 401K plans, investments, annuities, and more. There have been a number of changes over the past few years, particularly as they relate to health care. Know what you are entitled to and what you can depend upon.

3. Create a plan for health care and long-term care coverage and determine costs associated with these areas. Don't forget about the high cost of prescription drugs.

4. Consider how any emergency expenses will be handled and prepare a contingency plan to handle this.

5. Look at your own family. Are you likely to be more or less financially responsible for other family members during your retirement years?

FINDING THE RETIREMENT PLACE OF YOUR DREAMS

B*aby boomers—the generation on the cusp of retirement— are proactively seeking their individually perfect retirement location, and their standards are high. How do you go about figuring out if you're making the right decision? Here are some suggestions.*

1. *Expenses:* Check out the work options, housing prices, and tax rates for any place you're considering.

2. *Community:* Research the demographics of your location (go to the Census Bureau's Web site) to find out about your new neighbors. Visit the local Chamber of Commerce Web site as well, and pick up a copy of the local and regional newspapers to learn about issues, events, and other items of importance to residents.

3. *Health and Wellness:* Find out how far away the best hospital or medical center is, and check that institution to make sure it has the most up-to-date facilities and staff. Web sites devoted to alternative health can help you make sure you'll have easy access to practitioners.

4. *Learning and Education:* Investigate the local opportunities for continuing education, especially degree-granting institutions. Access to a major university will bring a broad range of benefits to older local residents beyond classes and courses.

5. *Transportation:* Make sure you have access to reliable local public transportation: You won't want to have to drive everywhere. Weigh the advantages and disadvantages of relocating far from a major airport hub or rail line.

6. *Environment:* Some people can't live without the change of seasons; others have had enough of snow and ice, or heat and rain. Make sure you know what you're getting into, weather-wise. While you're at it, check out any new location for the kind of details that are rarely mentioned by real estate agents: Superfund cleanup sites, nuclear power plants, plutonium storage facilities, or wilderness acreage that's not legally protected.

7. *Quality-of-Life Details:* What enhances your life? Don't assume your new place will offer those little things that mean a lot to you; great cappuccino, a cozy used book store, inspiring yarn shop, spicy Indian food, enticing hiking trail, or restful public garden. Make your list of small-but-essential features, and check them off as you find them.

FIND WHAT YOU NEED ONLINE

There's a wealth of information on the Web about any activity you may want to investigate. Try these sites to start; they'll lead you to more.

Travel/Volunteerism
www.Iesc.org (economic development projects)
www.Peacecorps.org
www.Globalvolunteers.org
www.Habitat.org (Habitat for Humanity)

Volunteerism
www.Civicventures.org
www.Pointsoflight.org
www.Experiencecorps.org
www.Score.org
www.Americorps.org

Travel
www.Seniorshomeexchange.com
www.Grandtrvl.com

Financial
www.401Khelpcenter.com

Education
www.elderhostel.org
www.seniornet.org
usm.maine.edu/olli/national

Writing
www.satw.org (a travel writing Web site)
www.writermag.com

For Women
www.womansage.com
www.redhatsociety.org
www.nwhn.org
www.thetransitionnetwork.com

Genealogy
www.gengateway.com
www.ellisisland.org
www.ancestry.com

Work
www.seniorjobbank.com
www.monster.com
www.hotjobs.com
www.elance.com
www.freelance.com

General Interest

www.demko.com (for and about boomers and zoomers)

www.ncoa.org

www.asaging.org

www.ageworks.com

www.aarp.org

Sites to Remember

_____

_____

_____

_____

_____

SPECIAL THANKS

Thanks to our intrepid "headhunters" for going out to find so many respondents from around the country with interesting advice to share:

Jamie Allen, Chief Headhunter

Andrea Fine
Andrea Syrtash
Beshaleba Rodell
Connie Farrow
Helen Bond
Jen Hinger
Jennifer Bright
  Reich

Jenny McNeill-
  Brown
Jody Shenn
Kazz Regelman
Ken McCarthy
Laura Stevens
Linda Lincoln
Lisa Jaffe Hubbell

Natasha
  Lambropoulos
Nicole Colangelo-
  Lessin
Patricia Woods
Shannon Hurd

Thanks, too, to our editorial adviser Anne Kostick. And thanks to our assistant, Miri Greidi, for her yeoman's work at keeping us all organized. The real credit for this book, of course, goes to all the people whose experiences and collective wisdom make up this guide. There are too many of you to thank individually, but you know who you are.

CREDITS

Page 5   *www.RetirementPlanner.org.*

Page 6   "The State of Retirement Planning," by Emily
            Brandon, *US News and World Report* online,
            March 26, 2006.

Page 9   "65+ in the United States: 2005," by Wan He,
            Manisha Sengupta, Victoria A. Velkoff, and
            Kimberly A. DeBarros, U.S. Department of
            Health and Human Services and U.S.
            Department of Commerce, December 2005.

Page 29   "Prime Time: Follow these steps to a happy
            retirement," by Emily Brandon, *US News and
            World Report* online, February 22, 2006.

Page 33   "Today's Retirement Journey: Forget those
            stereotypes."

Page 37   "Today's Retirement Journey: Forget those
            stereotypes."

Page 50   "65+ in the United States: 2005."

Page 53   *www.RetirementPlanner.org.*

Page 55   "65+ in the United States: 2005."

Page 59   *www.BestRetirementSpots.com.*

Page 68   "Prime Time: Follow these steps to a happy
            retirement."

Page 76   "Prepare your marriage for retirement,"
            www.msnbc.msn.com.

Page 71   *www.RetirementPlanner.org.*

Page 87   "65+ in the United States: 2005."

Page 88   "Good Riddance to the Rat Race: Today's
            retirees are looking for the good life in all the
            small places," by Nisha Ramachandran, *US
            News and World Report*, June 13, 2005.

Page 93   *www.RetirementPlanner.org.*
Page 94   *www.RetirementPlanner.org.*
Page 101   *www.AARP.org.*
Page 103   *www.AARP.org.*
Page 113   *www.HobbyWorld.com*
Page 119   *www.SeniorNet.org.*
Page 139   "Today's Retirement Journey: Forget those stereotypes."
Page 140   Healthy Retirement Tips, *US News and World Report* online, June 13, 2005.
Page 144   *www.AARP.org.*
Page 153   "Today's Retirement Journey: Forget those stereotypes."
Page 158   "Today's Retirement Journey: Forget those stereotypes."
Page 161   *www.RetirementPlanner.org.*
Page 162   "Prime Time: Follow these steps to a happy retirement."
Page 167   "Models for Measuring Quality of Life: Implications for Human-animal Interaction Research," Barofsky, I., and A. Rown, 1988.

Praise for HUNDREDS OF HEADS® *Guides:*

"Hundreds of Heads is an innovative publishing house...Its entertaining and informative 'How To Survive ...' series takes a different approach to offering advice. Thousands of people around the nation were asked for their firsthand experiences and real-life tips in six of life's arenas. Think 'Chicken Soup' meets 'Zagats,' says a press release, and rightfully so."

—ALLEN O. PIERLEONI
"BETWEEN THE LINES," THE SACRAMENTO BEE

"A concept that will be ... a huge seller and a great help to people. I firmly believe that today's readers want sound bytes of information, not tomes. Your series will most definitely be the next 'Chicken Soup.'"

—CYNTHIA BRIAN
TV/RADIO PERSONALITY, BEST SELLING AUTHOR: CHICKEN SOUP FOR THE GARDENER'S SOUL; BE THE STAR YOU ARE!; THE BUSINESS OF SHOW BUSINESS

"Move over, 'Dummies'.... Can that 'Chicken Soup!' Hundreds of Heads are on the march to your local bookstore!"

—ELIZABETH HOPKINS
KFNX (PHOENIX) RADIO HOST, THINKING OUTSIDE THE BOX

"The series ... could be described as 'Chicken Soup for the Soul' meets 'Worst Case Scenario.'"

—RACHEL TOBIN RAMOS
ATLANTA BUSINESS CHRONICLE

Praise for other titles in the HUNDREDS OF HEADS® *series:*

HOW TO LOSE 9,000 LBS. (OR LESS)

"Informative and entertaining ... a must-read if you have ever struggled with the delicate 'D' word."

—ZORA ANDRICH
REALITY SHOW CONTESTANT

"Something here may get you through a hard patch or help you lose those final few pounds."

—JIM KIEST
SAN ANTONIO EXPRESS-NEWS

HOW TO SURVIVE YOUR MARRIAGE

"I love this book!"

—DONNA BRITT
HOST, LIFETIME RADIO

"Reader-friendly and packed full of good advice. They should hand this out at the marriage license counter!"

—BOB NACHSHIN
CELEBRITY DIVORCE ATTORNEY AND CO-AUTHOR OF
I DO, YOU DO . . . BUT JUST SIGN HERE

"Useful marriage advice for once. This is not your typical New Age marriage manual full of psychobabble like 'Keep the lines of communication open.'"

—LAURI GITHENS HATCH
GANNETT NEWS SERVICE/ROCHESTER DEMOCRAT & CHRONICLE

HOW TO SURVIVE A MOVE

"Presented in tidbits that are easy to digest when you're more concerned with packing boxes than spending hours reading a book."

—SAN DIEGO TRIBUNE

"*How to Survive A Move* is full of common-sense ideas and moving experiences from everyday people. I have been in the moving industry for 22 years and I was surprised at all the new ideas I learned from your book!"

—FRED WALLACE
PRESIDENT, ONE BIG MAN & ONE BIG TRUCK MOVING COMPANY

HOW TO SURVIVE DATING

"Rated one of the Top 10 Dating Books."

—ABOUT.COM

"Invaluable advice ... If I had read this book before I made my movie, it would have been only *10 Dates*."

—MYLES BERKOWITZ, FILMMAKER
WROTE, DIRECTED AND WENT OUT ON *20 DATES* FOR FOX SEARCHLIGHT

"Great, varied advice, in capsule form, from the people who should know—those who've dated and lived to tell the tale."

—SALON.COM

HOW TO SURVIVE YOUR FRESHMAN YEAR

"This book proves that all of us are smarter than one of us."

——JOHN KATZMAN
FOUNDER AND CEO, PRINCETON REVIEW

"Voted in the Top 40 Young Adults Nonfiction books."

——PENNSYLVANIA SCHOOL LIBRARIANS ASSOCIATION

"This cool new book ... helps new college students get a head start on having a great time and making the most of this new and exciting experience."

——COLLEGE OUTLOOK

HOW TO SURVIVE YOUR TEENAGER

"Parents of teens and parents of kids approaching those years will find wisdom on each page ... provides insight, humor, and empathy ..."

——FOREWORD MAGAZINE

"With warmth, humor and 'I've been there' compassion, editors Gluck and Rosenfeld have turned the ordinary experiences and struggles of parents into bits of compact wisdom that are easy to pick up and use straightaway. I especially liked this book's many examples of how to survive (and even thrive) while living under the same roof as your teen."

——JACLYNN MORRIS, M.ED.
CO-AUTHOR OF *I'M RIGHT. YOU'RE WRONG. NOW WHAT?*
AND *FROM ME TO YOU*

HOW TO SURVIVE YOUR BABY'S FIRST YEAR

"What to read when you're reading the other baby books. The perfect companion for your first-year baby experience."

—SUSAN REINGOLD, M.A.
EDUCATOR

"*How to Survive Your Baby's First Year* ... offers tried-and-true methods of baby care and plenty of insight to the most fretted about parenting topics ..."

—*BOOKVIEWS*

"Full of real-life ideas and tips. If you love superb resource books for being the best parent you can be, you'll love *How to Survive Your Baby's First Year.*"

—ERIN BROWN CONROY, M.A.
AUTHOR, COLUMNIST, MOTHER OF TWELVE, AND CREATOR OF
TOTALLYFITMOM.COM

"The Hundreds of Heads folks have done it again! Literally hundreds of moms and dads from all over offer their nuggets of wisdom—some sweet, some funny, all smart—on giving birth, coming home and bringing up baby."

—ANDREA SARVADY
AUTHOR OF *BABY GAMI*

"YOU CAN KEEP THE DAMN CHINA!"

"If you're holding this book, it's probably because you're contemplating divorce or are in the process of one. Keep going: open the cover. By the last pages, you'll be be rid of one emotion you've felt for too long—shame—and in its place will bloom something you haven't felt in too long—hope."

— LAURI GITHENS HATCH
GANNETT NEWS SERVICE/ROCHESTER DEMOCRAT & CHRONICLE

HOW TO SURVIVE THE REAL WORLD

"Stories, tips, and advice from hundreds of college grads who found out what It takes to survive in the real world."

— WENDY ZANG
KNIGHT RIDDER/TRIBUNE NEWS SERVICE

"Perfect gift for the newly minted college graduates on your list."

— FRAN HAWK
THE POST AND COURIER (CHARLESTON, SC)

HELP YOUR FRIENDS SURVIVE!

Order extra copies of *How to Love Your Retirement,* or one of our other books.

Please send me:

_____ copies of *How to Love Your Retirement* (@$13.95)
_____ copies of *How to Survive the Real World* (@$13.95)
_____ copies of *Where to Seat Aunt Edna* (@$13.95)
_____ copies of *"You Can Keep the Damn China!"* (@$13.95)
_____ copies of *How to Lose 9,000 Lbs. (or Less)* (@$13.95)
_____ copies of *How to Survive Your Teenager* (@$13.95)
_____ copies of *How to Survive a Move* (@$13.95)
_____ copies of *How to Survive Your Marriage* (@$13.95)
_____ copies of *How to Survive Your Baby's First Year* (@$12.95)
_____ copies of *How to Survive Dating* (@$12.95)
_____ copies of *How to Survive Your Freshman Year* (@$13.95)

Please add $3.00 for shipping and handling for one book, and $1.00 for each additional book. Georgia residents add 4% sales tax. Kansas residents add 5.3% sales tax. Payment must accompany orders. Please allow three weeks for delivery.

My check for $_____ is enclosed.
Please charge my __ Visa __ MasterCard __ American Express

Name _____
Organization _____
Address _____
City/State/Zip _____
Phone _____E-mail _____
Credit card # _____
Exp. Date _____Signature _____
Please make checks payable to HUNDREDS OF HEADS Books, LLC

Please fax to 212-937-2220 or mail to:

HUNDREDS OF HEADS BOOKS, LLC
#230
2221 Peachtree Road, Suite D
Atlanta, Georgia 30309

HELP WRITE THE NEXT HUNDREDS OF HEADS® GUIDE!

Tell us your story about a life experience and what lesson you learned from it. If we use your story in one of our books, we'll send you a free copy. Use this card or visit **www.hundredsofheads.com**.

Here's my story/advice about

☐ **COLLEGE** (name of college: _____ first choice? _____)

☐ **FINDING A JOB** (length of job search: _____)

☐ **OTHER TOPIC** (you pick) _____

Name: _____City/State: _____

☐ Use my name ☐ Use my initials only ☐ Anonymous
(Note: Your entry in the book may also include city/state and the descriptive information above.)

_____
Signature

How should we contact you *(this will not be published or shared)*:

e-mail: _____ other: _____

Please fax to 212-937-2220 or mail to:

HUNDREDS OF HEADS BOOKS, LLC
#230, 2221 Peachtree Road, Suite D
Atlanta, Georgia 30309

Your story/advice:

_____

_____

_____

_____

_____

_____

_____

_____

_____

_____

VISIT WWW.HUNDREDSOFHEADS.COM

Do you have something interesting to say about marriage, your in-laws, dieting, holding a job, or one of life's other challenges?

Help humanity—share your story!

Get published in our next book!

Find out about the upcoming titles in the HUNDREDS OF HEADS® survival guide series!

Read up-to-the-minute advice on many of life's challenges!

Sign up to become an interviewer for one of the next HUNDREDS OF HEADS® survival guides!

Visit www.hundredsofheads.com today!

ABOUT THE EDITORS

BARBARA LYNN WAXMAN, M.S., M.P.A., is an executive and life transition coach, trainer and speaker. She is a gerontologist and has worked in the field of aging for the past 20 years. Barbara founded The Odyssey Group in 2005 to guide others with compassion, honesty and a light heart as they pursue meaningful changes in their lives. Barbara lives outside of San Francisco, California.

ROBERT A. MENDELSON, M.D., F.A.A.P., is a 71-year-old retired pediatrician. At age 65 he cut back his practice and dropped the really hard stuff, such as night call and working weekends. He retired completely at age 70 to be a caregiver for his wife, who developed leukemia and has required two stem-cell transplants. With his wife, he co-authored a book on parenting and contributed a chapter to the American Academy of Pediatrics parenting book. He started preparing for financial retirement in his 30s. Bob plays tennis a lot and golf a little and enjoys his four children and eight grandchildren. He lives in Portland, Oregon, rated one of the best cities in the U.S. for retirement.